Distant Mirrors
America as a Foreign Culture

Wadsworth books of related interest

Richard de Mille: The Don Juan Papers: Further Castaneda Controversies

Philip R. DeVita: The Humbled Anthropologist: Tales from the Pacific

Philip R. DeVita: The Naked Anthropologist: Tales from Around the World

Conrad Phillip Kottak: Prime-Time Society: An Anthropological Analysis of Television and Culture

Mac Marshall and Leslie B. Marshall: Silent Voices Speak: Women and Prohibition in Truk

R. Jon McGee: Life, Ritual, and Religion Among the Lacandon Maya

Serena Nanda: Neither Man nor Woman: The Hijras of India

Alice Pomponio: Seagulls Don't Fly Into the Bush: Cultural Identity and Development in Melanesia

Distant Mirrors
America as a Foreign Culture

Edited by

Philip R. DeVita
State University of New York, Plattsburgh

James D. Armstrong
State University of New York, Plattsburgh

Wadsworth Publishing Company
Belmont California
A Division of Wadsworth, Inc.

Anthropology Editor: *Peggy Adams*
Editorial Assistant: *Dorothy Zinky*
Production Editor: *Deborah Cogan*
Managing Designer: *Andrew Ogus*
Print Buyer: *Randy Hurst*
Permissions Editor: *Robert Kauser*
Copy Editor: *Melissa Andrews*
Cover Designer: *Andrew Ogus*
Cover Illustrator: *Amy Wasserman*
Compositor: *Bookends Typesetting*
Printer: *Malloy Lithographing, Inc.*

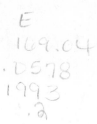

4 5 6 7 8 9 10—97 96 95 94

Printed in the United States of America

Library of Congress Cataloging-in-Publication Data

Distant mirrors: America as a foreign culture / [compiled by] Philip
  R. DeVita, James D. Armstrong.
    p. cm.
  Includes bibliographical references.
  ISBN 0-534-17676-3
    1. United States—Social life and customs—1971– —Foreign public
opinion. 2. United States—Popular culture—Foreign public opinion.
I. DeVita, Philip R., 1932– . II. Armstrong, James D., 1948– .
E169.04.D578 1993
306.4′0973—dc20   92-28875

 Contents

An anthropologist from Portugal examines such cultural traits as informal language use, social life, body ritual, and football, and offers critical insights into customs that Americans take for granted.

Professor Kim, a scholar in the area of intercultural communication and communication theory, has spent more than twenty years in the United States. In a letter written to a close friend from his native country of South Korea, he speaks entertainingly of American approaches to privacy, manners, sexual mores, individuality, and interpersonal relationships.

A Polish sociologist compares his European idea of the "city" to what he discovered in the United States. He discusses the immediate and informal cordiality of Americans, the prevalence of urban anonymity, and the naturalness of violence, patriotism, education, ethnocentrism, and potluck dinners.

After many years as a resident analyst of American culture, Professor Varenne reflects on differing interpretations of the experiences he had when he came to this country as a graduate student from France. Others thought he was going through culture shock, but he viewed his experiences quite differently.

By relating a variety of his encounters with Americans, Professor Huang shows how such experiences can lead to greater understanding of one's own culture. He emphasizes that even anthropologists can have difficulty freeing themselves from their assumptions about their own culture.

From the point of view of a scholar raised in Thailand, Americans appear open and immediately friendly in their greetings. But if one looks more closely, these greetings seem more superficial and ritualized, hiding the more important aspects of American cultural values.

Professor Ojeda, now a scholar in anthropology and linguistics, describes her initial difficulty in adjusting to some American customs as a young student on her first visit to America. Years later, in returning to the United States with her daughter, she faced a crucial conflict between American values and the more respectful values of her own Philippine traditions.

A linguistics scholar from Zaire examines the American system of person-to-person address, contrasting the informality of American forms of address with the formalized system used in his native country.

Excerpts from her diary recount a French anthropologist's reflections on the New York City neighborhood she lived in after five years in the Australian Outback. She describes a neighborhood characterized by poverty, homelessness, and drug-dealing, as well as the culture of the neighboring, wealthier residents of "The City."

When Professor Cerroni-Long, an Asian scholar from Italy, visited Japan, she discovered that intellectual preparation does not protect one from culture shock. She tells how the conscious application of cultural anthropological techniques provided her with the foundations for both survival and understanding.

In a thought-provoking critique, Professor Pinxten discusses his view of the academic system as a model of the corporate world, and poignantly discusses the differences between European and American ethnographic methodologies and the decline of American intellectualism.

Drawing on her background in both Israel and France, a scholar
of social anthropology describes coming to grips with gender encounters in the context of academic culture at a southern
university.

The author of this essay looks at how American homeowners both
resist and come to terms with the ownership of common property,
contrasting the private cluster home neighborhood where he did
his fieldwork with his experience in urban China. He clearly articulates the barriers that American individualism can create for the
development of community.

Professor Drechsel, an anthropologist who was born in Switzerland,
discusses the American tendency to view ourselves as culturally
European. Using both his European background and his long-term
familiarity with the United States, he argues convincingly that there
is a unique American culture strongly influenced by non-European
sources, especially the Native American culture.

Understanding Ourselves: Introductory Remarks for the Student and the General Reader

Had Alexis de Tocqueville been American instead of French, his unusually perceptive 1835 observations on American life would probably have been unremarkable. They are acutely perceptive precisely because he brought to them what no American could: the startling freshness of an outsider's perspective.

This book carries that idea one step further. It brings together the perspectives of 14 outsiders, anthropologists and other scholars from other countries who have studied America as a foreign culture.

Anthropology has a long history of concern with the "other," the different, the strange. By developing a better understanding of others and their cultures, we gain a comparative perspective for more lucidly understanding ourselves and our own immediate world. Unfortunately, the ethnographic laboratory today differs radically from the earlier days of doing fieldwork among seemingly pristine peoples in remote and exotic places. The global village is a fact, and the romantic vision of ethnographic adventure among remote and untouched peoples is gone. The Pacific Island cultures, for example, are rapidly and sadly becoming soda-pop and tinned-fish wastelands. Anthropologists face this model almost everywhere we turn.

We are therefore compelled to look closer to home for the strangeness or the similarities that we seek. Increasingly, anthropologists turn to the "alien" pockets within our own culture.

It is difficult, however, for a social scientist to fully appreciate the strangeness and wonder of his or her own culture. The cultural assumptions we grow up with are powerful. As insiders—speaking the language, following the accepted patterns of behavior, being embedded in a particular way of life—we tend to take most aspects of our own social action for granted. We see our own routine behavior as uninteresting. We forget to ask the questions that reveal our own culture's underlying values and beliefs. In short, when looking at ourselves, our own mirrors may be clouded.

That is where this book comes in. It provides other mirrors, other reflections. Outsiders, having grown up in other cultures, won't take as much for granted about our behavior as we do. They will not share our assumptions about what is appropriate and accepted. They will attend to different things and ask different questions than we would. They will interpret our routine behavior in other ways and see significance in what for us seems meaningless. They will provide other ways of understanding how American behavior is culturally constructed. Their lack of both emotional involvement and embeddedness in the contexts they encounter—and, hence, the freshness of their viewpoints—will provide us with different understandings than we can gain by ourselves.

This is not to say that insiders studying themselves don't have advantages. Certainly our self-knowledge and self-awareness give us a head start in studying ourselves. But when cultural insiders set out to study their own culture, they must first lose their familiarity with it and distance themselves from it. Cultural outsiders, by virtue of their otherness, don't have to manufacture distance. It is already there. Thus, they are keenly aware of what warrants explanation. In making sense out of what appears strange, outsiders can easily read between the cultural lines and contextualize our behavior in a broader comparative perspective. So what they might miss through lack of awareness is more than compensated for by their relative lack of familiarity and ready access to comparison.

To create this collection, we asked anthropologists from many areas of the world to write essays. We told them that we wanted literate insights into everyday American life, with no holds barred. Articles could be humorous, caustic, critical—but not heavily theoretical and certainly not written in the traditional academic style of journal articles. We asked that the authors give first-person accounts of their personal experiences.

We are most grateful to those authors who have made this volume possible as well as to those authors who, for whatever reasons, are not included here. Of the authors who are included, about half are non-Westerners. Some authors worked in the United States for only a brief time; others have lived in the United States for a number of years.

This is not, of course, the first attempt to use foreign viewpoints to look at American culture. Indeed, several of the contributors to this collection are among the growing number of foreign scholars who have written eloquently about American culture. But this is one of the few books that brings together the perspectives of anthropologists from a variety of homelands in a single volume.

While reading these articles, consider the degree to which you agree or disagree with each author's conclusions. For example, is American culture truly distinct from European culture, as Emanuel Dreschel argues? Are Americans really intolerant of ambiguity in interpersonal relations, as Rahel Wasserfall asserts? Do the authors' assertions apply to all Americans or only to smaller segments of the population? Are all Americans neighborly strangers, or is the lack of involvement in neighbors' lives limited to the cluster home projects that Honggang Yang describes? What is it about Thai childrearing that causes Poranee Natadecha-Sponsel to react to the independence of American children the way she does? Does Francisco Martins Ramos's European background produce a substantially different reading of American cultural practices than do Huang Shu-min's or Jin K. Kim's Asian perspectives?

Most of what students read and hear in introductory cultural anthropology courses comes from the perspective of American anthropologists who have studied "strangers." That one-sidedness deserves some correction. This book is a step in that direction. It is based on the belief that we can see ourselves in a more critically clear light when we hear from those who consider *us* the strangers.

Phil DeVita and James Armstrong
Plattsburgh, New York

Acknowledgments

There are a number of people who deserve our thanks. First, we would like to thank all the contributing authors for their patience with us and for their cooperation on this project. Both of us recognize that our associations with a number of other non-Americans, who have shared their insights about our culture, helped us to realize the importance of this project. Many thanks to James Clifton, who encouraged Phil DeVita to put this collection together. Our close friend and colleague Richard Robbins read and commented on all of the manuscripts, and often reinforced our commitment to this project. His concerns, enthusiasm, and insights were important to both of us. Peggy Adams of Wadsworth Publishing Company is to be thanked for again taking on a nontraditional project, as is Deborah Cogan, for this, her third exercise in so professionally nurturing another of DeVita's projects to completion.

We also appreciate the comments of colleagues who reviewed the manuscript as a whole: Stephen Childs, Valdosta State College; Jon McGee, Southwest Texas State University; Edwin Segal, University of Louisville.

Phil DeVita and James Armstrong
Plattsburgh, New York

Outsiders' Reflections on Being American: Some Pedagogical Concerns

JAMES ARMSTRONG

When Phil DeVita asked me to collaborate on a collection of articles by foreign anthropologists on the United States, I was immediately reminded of a visit that Mehdy Soroya made to our college several years ago. Professor Soroya is an Iranian anthropologist and retired chair of the Anthropology faculty at Teheran University. During his visit he most graciously agreed to share his reflections on American culture from the perspective of an experienced outsider. He explained how his experiences as a social psychology graduate student at an American university led him to a career as a cultural anthropologist. He focused on those aspects of American life that he found strange: an emphasis on equality but a tolerance for inequality, arrogance tempered by a high degree of naiveté, and a desire to avoid controversy. As he turned from subject to subject, he situated himself and his Iranian experience in his discourse to allow the audience to understand how his point of view developed. By doing so he actively engaged us in a conversation about ourselves. He forced us to make comparisons, to reflect, to take the point of view of the other. In the process he made us understand ourselves better. He gave substance to some of the complaints of those of us who were generally critical of American society and culture. He raised the hackles of others who viewed the American way as sacrosanct. Even for the most ethnocentric, he created that discomfort that leads to doubt and questioning. In recalling his talk, I could immediately see the value of a volume by others about us, and I was pleased to be able to participate in its creation.

Of course this idea isn't particularly original, nor is this volume the first attempt to bring foreign scrutiny to bear on American culture, as anyone who has read Alexis de Tocqueville is sure to know. In American cultural anthropology, Franz Boas encouraged the training of non-Western anthropologists, while Alfred Kroeber helped arrange for a Chinese anthropologist, Li An-Che, to study the Zuni (1937). Significantly, Li's findings were, on a number of issues, at odds with what American researchers had written about the Zuni. As a means of reconciling the differences, Li argued that observers will attend to differing aspects of cultural patterns, depending on their background. Furthermore, Li's interpretation, informed by his Chinese perspective, provided insights into the cultural assumptions American researchers used to reach their conclusions with respect to childrearing and leadership among the Zuni.

Another Chinese anthropologist, Francis L. K. Hsu, perhaps the most prolific foreign-born anthropological analyst of American culture, framed his research with his background in China and India (1953, 1963). His characterization of Americans as individual centered (1963) with a core value on self-reliance (1972) gains in significance as time passes. As an illustration, one needs only to consider *Habits of the Heart,* the study of the relationship of the individual American to American society in which Bellah and his coauthors (1985) extensively restate Hsu's earlier conclusions about our core values. Furthermore, the conscious grounding of Hsu's conclusion in comparison to others is precisely the kind of approach we encouraged the authors of the articles in this volume to take.

More recently there have been a number of other non-Americans who have productively studied and eloquently written about aspects of American culture and about the issues surrounding others studying Americans. For example, John Ogbu, a Nigerian (Ibo) (1974, 1978), has written extensively and critically about minority schooling in the United States. French-born anthropologist Hervé Varenne (1977, 1983), who has contributed an article to this volume, has also written about American high school education and everyday life. Choong Soon Kim (1977), a Korean, has written about his experiences as an Asian anthropologist doing fieldwork in a variety of contexts in the southern part of the United States. His recent article in *Current Anthropology* (1990) discusses many of the advantages and disadvantages of outsiders working in this culture. It is my hope that this body of literature will continue to grow and that eventually it will produce the kind of "stretching of the assumptions and categories" by others that Keesing and Keesing (1971:370) called for.

From the onset of this project, it seemed to me that the main advantage of outsiders' reflections on us is that those who have grown up in other cultures will have different assumptions about what is appropriate. Because their expectations about what should occur in particular cultural contexts will often be different from what actually does occur, they will have different questions about what they experience in those contexts than an insider would. The questions they ask quite possibly will lead to insightful interpretations of American behavior. I am not denying that insiders' prior knowledge of the cultural system is sometimes an advantage in research, and I know that it is possible for insiders to escape the trap of taking too much for granted. Still, outsiders will often attend to different things, find new meanings in what is routine to us, and provide other ways of understanding how American behavior is culturally constructed.

Some might suggest that the hegemony of the Western worldview in higher education and in the anthropological training of almost all anthropologists will reduce the differences among us to the extent that we all see the world in much the same way. Indeed, there may be some truth in this assertion, at least as far as theory and method are concerned. But the cultural assumptions that one grows up with are powerful. Thus, even if becoming anthropologists has entailed some acculturation for them, others won't take as much for granted about our behavior as we do.

It isn't just that others, even European others, have different assumptions about what is appropriate or inappropriate, good or bad, sacred or profane, but also that others automatically bring both distance and comparison to bear in their attempts to understand us. Even when members of the same culture, cultural insiders, study themselves, it is a common procedure to manufacture distance and to use comparison and contrast to produce explanation. For example, Tamar Katriel, an Israeli anthropologist who has written extensively about her own culture, writes of "the movement of de-familiarization" where the mundane "shed their accustomed air of 'naturalness' and become interpretive sites for the exploration of cultural sense" (1991:2). She claims the process of defamiliarization is basic to the ethnographic craft.

In another example, Constance Perin, in a recent book about neighbors in American suburbs, describes the process of distancing herself from the subject:

> To help me see between the lines by which I also live, before setting out for the field I tried to defamiliarize myself by visiting countries having high residential densities, where relations with neighbors were likely to be salient. . . . I wasn't trying to develop an ethnography of their neighbor relationships, but only to listen for issues that I might not have thought to consider, as well as for sheer differences in their lines and concepts. In turn, their experiences in, observations of, and questions about American concepts and practices were equally valuable in disorienting me. These travels were whetstones for sharpening my observations at home. (1988:6)

As Perin makes explicit, anthropologists who study their own culture must distance themselves from their object of study. Cultural outsiders, by virtue of their otherness, don't have to manufacture distance; it is already there. Thus, they are keenly aware of what warrants explanation.

In making sense out of the behavior of cultural others, it is common to try to anchor that behavior in our own experiences, to compare it to and contrast it with behaviors familiar to us. Although this process leads to some embarrassing fieldwork gaffes, even these can be revealing. In making sense out of what appears strange, outsiders can easily read between the cultural lines and contextualize our behavior in a broader comparative perspective. Thus, what they might miss through lack of awareness is more than compensated for by their relative lack of familiarity and ready access to comparison.

The pedagogical value of the other's perspective appealed to both Phil DeVita and me. We both teach introductory-level cultural anthropology courses to large numbers of students, and we both use ethnography as a mirror of American culture, albeit a complex and poorly understood one. We both agree that ethnography is not only a way of viewing others but also a way of understanding ourselves. The questions that students have about others, and the similarities and differences that they perceive in the behaviors of other peoples, can almost always be used to create self-reflection. We thought that we could encourage this cultural self-reflection produced by reading about others as we see them by providing students with the opportunity to read about Americans as others see us. In fact, it seems to me that a crucial first step for students learning to appreciate the cultures of others is developing the realization that they themselves live in a culturally constructed world. I am convinced that the "strangeness" in others can be made sense of only by first realizing the strangeness in ourselves. Thus, the reflectiveness that reading these articles should produce, the cultural self-awareness that we are aiming for, is a vital element in introductory anthropology courses.

Furthermore, we saw the introduction of other's perspectives as a small contribution to the decolonization of our discipline. Most of what students read and hear about in introductory cultural anthropology courses is from the perspective of an American anthropologist studying others, who are often the relatively powerless peoples of postcolonial societies. The one-sidedness of this process deserves some correction. At the same time, it is important to inject a degree of awareness about how cultural assumptions always affect the questions being asked and the interpretations being drawn. The self-conscious presence of the authors of these articles should generate this kind awareness for students. Our feeling is that we can stimulate reflection and produce a more critical understanding of our culture by providing students with outsider views of American culture. This process of simultaneously looking outward and looking inward should enhance our understanding of others and of ourselves.

Because each article is prefaced with a brief introduction intended to cue the attention of the reader, I will not review the articles in much detail here. But I would like to point to some of the issues that might be used to spark classroom discussion about these articles and to enhance their value for students. This collection might remind some of Horace Miner's "Body Ritual Among the Nacirema" (1956), in which he exoticized American lavatory practices, among other things, by assuming an "objective," outsider-like perspective. One point of the article, whether we view it as a spoof or as a critical representation of mundane, secular American ritual, is that others' interpretations of our behavior can be different from our own. It might be a worthwhile exercise to have students read this article and discuss it before reading this colleciton. One central point of a discussion of "Body Ritual" (or of any of the articles in this collection for that matter) should be the sources of the author's interpretations. In addition, using "Body Ritual" will key students' attention to issues of authenticity, credibility, and ethnocentrism.

The essays should raise a number of valuable questions for classroom discussions. Some of these questions were mentioned in the previous section, "Understanding Ourselves: Introductory Remarks for the Student and General Reader." Because all of these essays are, to varying degrees, critical of us, readers should also be prepared to defend and challenge these criticisms.

The main pedagogical goal of this book is to create new ways for predominantly American readers to understand their own culture. Because we saw this as a book directed primarily at an audience of undergraduate students, we wanted it to be one that would be appealing for them to read. To that end we instructed the authors to personalize their accounts and to avoid overly theoretical or technical analyses. Especially important was having the authors situate *themselves* in their articles, both to make the articles more personal and to allow students to understand the experiences that led to the authors' conclusions. Thus, we were interested in having subject matter that was familiar to students—that is, everyday life in a setting they know—interpreted by anthropologists who did not necessarily share the same worldview assumptions as the readers but with whom readers could identify. Students should learn to appreciate that the perspectives of others constitute an indispensable ingredient in the development of a critical understanding of themselves. These essays, given the accessible and personal ways in which they are written along with the familiarity of the subject matter, are excellent means for encouraging reflectiveness and critical awareness in our students.

A NOTE ON ORGANIZATION

Our original inclination in arranging the articles was to categorize them by the standard subjects, or some subset of those subjects, covered in an introductory cultural anthropology course. We resisted this inclination for several reasons. First, not all the articles lend themselves to easy classification. Most of them in fact deal with more than one theme and could not easily be assigned to a single category. Second, our experience as teachers tells us that the organization of a collection of articles usually has little impact on how they are used in practice. I always deviate from the structure of the books I use in my courses. Our sense is that most instructors will pick and choose articles in the order that best suits their purposes. Finally, we are not convinced that the subject-oriented approach to teaching introductory courses in anthropology is best. Organizing these articles by subject matter, if we could agree on their classification, would serve to reinforce a habit in the discipline that we view as having negative pedagogical repercussions. The authors did not write these articles about particular subjects. They wrote them about coming to terms with a new cultural system, about solving research problems, about their dilemmas in understanding us. To pigeonhole these articles would put us in the position of partially constructing their meaning for the readers.

REFERENCES CITED

BELLAH, ROBERT N., RICHARD MADSEN, WILLIAM SULLIVAN, ANN SWIDLER, AND STEVEN TIPTON
1985   Habits of the Heart: Individualism and Commitment in American Life. Berkeley: University of California Press.

HSU, FRANCIS L. K.
1953   American and Chinese: Two Ways of Life. New York: Henry Schuman.
1963   Clan, Caste, and Club. Princeton, NJ: D. Van Nostrand Co.
1972   American Core Value and National Character. *In* Psychological Anthropology. F. L. K. Hsu, ed. Pp. 214–262. Cambridge: Schenkman.

KATRIEL, TAMAR
1991   Communal Webs: Communication and Culture in Contemporary Israel. Albany: State University of New York Press.

KEESING, ROGER M., AND FELIX KEESING
1971   New Perspectives in Cultural Anthropology. New York: Holt.

KIM, CHOONG SOON
1977   An Asian Anthropologist in the South: Field Experiences with Blacks, Indians, and Whites. Knoxville: University of Tennessee Press.
1990   The Role of the Non-Western Anthropologist Reconsidered: Illusion versus Reality. Current Anthropology 31:196–201.

LI AN-CHE
1937   Zuni: Some Observations and Queries. American Anthropologist 39:62–76.

MINER, HORACE
1956   Body Ritual Among the Nacirema. American Anthropologist 58:503–507.

OGBU, JOHN
1974   The Next Generation: An Ethnography of Education in an Urban Neighborhood. New York: Academic Press.

1978 Minority Education and Cast: The American System in Cross-Cultural Perspective. New York: Academic Press.

PERIN, CONSTANCE
1988 Belonging in America: Reading between the Lines. Madison: University of Wisconsin Press.

VARENNE, HERVE
1977 Americans Together: Structured Diversity in a Midwestern Town. New York: Teachers College Press.
1983 American School Language: Culturally Patterned Conflicts in a Suburban High School. New York: Irvington Publishers.

Distant Mirrors
America as a Foreign Culture

ONE

My American Glasses

FRANCISCO MARTINS RAMOS
University of Évora, Portugal

From a Portuguese perspective, Professor Ramos examines a few American cultural traits, such as informal language use, social life, body ritual, football, and that great American shrine, the bathroom. In the style of Horace Miner, the author offers lucid and critical insights into many of the customs that Americans take for granted.

Francisco Martins Ramos *is assistant professor of Anthropology at the University of Évora, in Portugal. He was raised in the Alentejo, a southern rural area of Portugal. He lived in Africa and visited the United States several times. He received his B.A. in Anthropology from the Technical University of Lisbon (1978) and will have earned his doctorate in Anthropology at the University of Évora before the publication of this volume.*

The following text is a humble reflection on American daily life, resulting from my contact with American society. I must say that a foreigner's careful look is not necessarily more refined, precise, and detailed than that of the indigenous people. As paradigmatic examples I recall the famous articles Ralph Linton (1936) and Horace Miner (1956) wrote on aspects of American cultural reality. Inspired by the brilliant words and original ideas transmitted by these authors, respectively, in "One Hundred Percent American" and "Body Ritual Among the Nacirema," I will present a critical view of some forms of behavior, phenomena, and attitudes within American daily life that raised my interest or shocked me.

Half a dozen visits to the United States (totaling about eight months) allow me some insight, simultaneously close and distant, and have led me to the present reflections. The title I have selected simply reflects a new perspective resulting from a new angle of observation.

These comments do not pretend to reduce or caricature American culture or Americans, and they are not, surely, meant to express any superiority on the part of the author. Thus, the *chiens de garde* (guard dogs) of ethnocentrism will be warned, since this is a perspective that wishes to emphasize the richness of cultural differences and of people's identity and singularity.

When I mention American culture, the idea of diversity and heterogeneity is implicit, which is the consequence of a varied number of cultural inputs from the most diverse origins. American culture is the result of a multicultural amalgam that has been consolidating itself through the years and that is in permanent evolution, with a rhythm and a dynamic that surprises a European point of view.

The ideas expressed in this article correspond not only to my own personal opinions but also to those of many colleagues and friends who gave me help and important information. I assume total responsibility for their contributions.

The United States has always exercised a strange attraction for the spirit of the Portuguese: first, as the land of quick success; second, as the cradle of democracy; third, as an unrestrained jungle of competition; and, finally, as the model to follow. Perhaps for these very reasons there has never existed in Portugal the deep anti-American sentiment that characterizes other well-known European and world situations.

Nowadays, America comes to us, fresh and quickly, at the hour of TV news, ritually and arithmetically. Radio news programs or TV reports give information and news about the American nation every day. But the situation was not always like this.

Thirty or forty years ago, what we knew about America was mythologically overemphasized in the letters of some Azorean relative.

What we knew about America came from cowboy films and documentary movies that filled our eyes with the skyscrapers of New York or the memories of Al Capone's peripeteias.

What we knew about America was part of another world, distant, unreachable, almost abstract.

In Portugal, however, what used to confuse us were the inconceivable episodes of racial segregation. In fact, the Portuguese still had one foot (and its heart) in Africa and did not easily accept this business of ethnic discrimination—we who have mixed ourselves with African, Asian, and Amerindian peoples in the seven corners of the world.

Each Portuguese who learned on school benches that America separated herself from the British Empire had a secret and inexplicable sensation of joy and satisfaction at knowing the English were defeated. Because of an ancient treaty signed in the fourteenth century, we had to bear the British after their help against the French Napoleonic invasions, and this agreement has functioned more to their benefit than to ours. Thus, nations of colonial vocation vibrate with these pretty little joys!

We cried for John Kennedy and Martin Luther King, citizens of humankind, and, still today, we are commonly surprised how Ronald Reagan could become president of the greatest nation in the world.

With the development of modern media technologies, with the increase and improvement of the means of transportation, with the implementation of exchange programs and visits, with the increase of reciprocal tourism, America is today very close to us, and her mythology is no longer incomprehensible. She now generates other myths.

La recherche du temps perdu (the search for the lost time) is for a middle-class American the search for a history and for European roots. For that reason, Europeans are not badly treated in America. As Octavio Paz has said, "The United States drown themselves in the challenges of conceiving a country" (Santos 1989:2). As Walt Whitman wrote, what has united Americans has not been a common history, which they did not have, but "the will to build a future: a common future where utopia blends with reality" (Santos 1989:3).

I first visited the United States in 1982. For five months I lived in Madison, Wisconsin, a state with rural characteristics, which I was comfortable with. The Alentejo Province, where I was born and raised, was also rural, as are many of the areas of my country that lack the rapid advances of industrialization.

Later, during other visits, I had the opportunity to visit Milwaukee, Chicago, Washington, D.C., New York, Phoenix, Los Angeles, Dallas, Boston, and San Francisco, areas that offered examples of the rich urban vocation of the American nation.

What surprises us as Europeans is the fact that Americans could have done in less than 150 years what it took centuries for us to do. For better or worse, in this duel of contradictions, the struggle is between the old Puritan morality and a new hedonism. The paradox is the democratic identity of the United States—a collective project—and the constantly growing individualistic trend.

A Portuguese citizen arrives in America, conscious of his or her rural extraction, and the first thing that he or she realizes is that America is not a big megalopolis. We feel perfectly integrated in the rural world of a state such as Wisconsin—with an economy based on the primary sector, with conservative political horizons as in the majority of rural societies.

A less observant visitor can lose himself or herself in the complexity of multiple and contradictory cultural traits. First, we become submersed in the imperialism of material culture, in terms of shape, space, and time. After this comes the invasion of cultural behavior traits.

Unexpectedly, the first thing I found strange, even bizarre, was the use and abuse of the word *nice*, both in formal conversations and in colloquial language. I participated in the following dialogue at a family party on Thanksgiving Day:

"Nice to meet you. What's your name?"
"Francisco."
"Oh, nice! Do you have a family?"

"Yes, I have two children. . . ."

"Very nice! Do you like America?"

"Yes, but . . ."

"That's very nice! Do you like our weather?"

"It's a little cold for me. . . ."

"But today is a nice day! By the way, did you watch the football game last night?"

"I did, but I don't understand American football. . . ."

"Oh, it's a pretty nice sport!"

Some hours later:

"Bye-bye, Francisco. It was nice to meet you. . . . Have a nice stay in the States."

In fact, the abuse of the word *nice* shocks the hearing of an attentive interlocutor and of the visitor who is interested in dominating the meandering of North American language. Either a certain mental laziness exists that generates a simplification of the linguistic process of communication, or the English language does not have the vocabulary and the semantic richness to avoid abusive repetitions. "Pretty nice" and "It's nice to be nice" are expressions that capture the extreme of what I am referring to.

An American woman who has been introduced to us always hesitates in shaking hands and is not prepared to be kissed, even by another woman. I presume that this attitude derives from educational rules or is a self-defense mechanism. The compliment normally is, "Hi! Nice to meet you!"

It is interesting to note the practical sense that Americans give to forms of address. They avoid the European or Portuguese formalities of titles: mister doctor, mister engineer, mister architect, and so on. In America, preferential treatment stresses the Christian name, which in Portugal is used only with the passage of time or between kin and friends. There is a difference between the practical meaning of social relations and the world of true formality.

In the States, social life is programmed to arrange a dinner, a party, a picnic, a visit, and so on. These are operations planned far ahead. Sociability is not improvised; it is highly programmatic, predictable, and repetitive.

America has no parallel in the cult of physical exercise: Gymnastics, athletics, and life in the open air are integral parts of the daily life of Americans of all ages. Physical exercise is just one more part of Miner's "body ritual."

American football, in spite of being a game of truly male orientation, also attracts women as spectators, fans, and strong participants in discussions about the game. Up to now, European women have not been attracted by European soccer at any level: participation, attendance at games, or club/team discussions.

Football is characterized by virility, difficulty, and risks and is considered to employ a combination of war and chess strategies. Such a combination of animation and subtlety and the equilibrium of the metaphor appease the American conscience against all those (Europeans) who consider American football an exercise in brutality.

When Portuguese citizens leave their native province and arrive in America, they are confronted with a series of strange situations. Some situations provoke laughter, and others are quite dramatic and embarrassing. Many situations generate stupefaction. As a matter of fact, Horace Miner (1956), who some time ago had already subtlely played with some traits of North American culture, called our attention to the characteristics of the bathroom, the true ceremonial center of body ritual. A Portuguese who visits the bathroom in the home of an American friend faces some puzzling situations. For example, in the bathrooms of more than twenty American couples that time and friendship have allowed me to know, in dozens of hotels, motels, dormitories, bus and train stations, restaurants, and bars, no two water taps are alike. Consequently, I have encountered great difficulties in turning the water on, in adjusting cold and hot water, in regulating the faucet pressure, and in stopping the flow. The problem is that the tap mechanisms can be put into action by the pressure of a forefinger on a generally hidden button, by turning a screw that we wouldn't think to turn, by moving an appurtenance considered to be ornamental, or by using a masked hook, a secondary metal arabesque, or an invisible pedal.

If from the taps we move to showers, baths, and toilets, it is easy to recognize the embarrassment of a common Portuguese who is forced to make a detailed preliminary study of the sanitary equipment, which the circumstances do not always permit. We perfectly understand Americans' exemplary obsession with bad smells, as we can verify through the shape of toilets and the volume of water they consume in restrooms. However, the paraphernalia, mechanisms, and equipment are so different as to constitute a labyrinth for the rural European Portuguese.

In public rest rooms, the Portuguese amateur in urbanities will certainly be quite surprised with a form of cultural behavior never dreamt of: The American who urinates in public initiates conversation with the partner at his side, even if he does not know the latter! Themes of these occasional dialogues are the weather, football, politics, and so on. We can guess at the forced pleasure of the Portuguese, who heretofore has regarded urination as a necessary physical function, not as a social occasion. The public restroom! Is it an extension of the bar room?

Next, I would like to comment on gastronomy. The first consideration is the diversity of American food, rich and varied as many others, as a form of cultural manifestation. In this case, the gastronomic contributions from different and distant cultures make American cuisine a true "melting pot," an opportune expression to describe so-called "ethnic" food. A Portuguese who has not traveled much will be faced with the dilemma of choice in a restaurant or at the supermarket. In fact, there are seemingly endless types of sauces, numerous varieties of bread, an immense number of different kinds of cheese, potatoes cooked in various ways, and so on. Another marvel is the fast-food system, which fits perfectly into the American way of life. Indeed, during week days, the fast-food system is oriented to the performance of work, in a real struggle against time.

My discussion of gastronomy would not be complete without reference to table etiquette. Americans normally use the knife very little but use the fork continually. Those of us who have been educated by the French bible of good manners at the table have always been told that it is good etiquette to use a fork and knife simultaneously: fork in the left hand, knife in the right. Thus, we find it difficult to accept as proper etiquette the use of the fork with the right hand, leaving the left hand under the table as a sign of good manners.

Speaking of manners, if an American cannot avoid belching in public (he burps and naturally apologizes), for a Portuguese this means a lack of good manners. However, the same Portuguese will be positively impressed with the kindness and amiability showed by American pedestrians or drivers, who are always willing to give the correct information any time it is requested. The paradox is that Americans think the same way about the Portuguese.

Whereas some differences amaze and delight us, others are true shocks. One difference is the idea of one's sharing a bedroom with an American woman, without being involved in sex. Indeed, it is normal and current among university students, participants at conferences, and friends to share a bedroom and a bed only for practical reasons. We can imagine how a Portuguese (or a Spaniard or an Italian) would conceive of such partition without generating conflict with his engraved honor as a Latin macho. Something that an American woman does, with the greatest naturalness, will be more than reason for a Latin man not to sleep a wink all night, if it should happen that he shares the same room only with the intent of having a good sleep and reducing expenses. The Latin caught in this trap will necessarily have his night replete with dreams, his imagination well fed, and a prolonged insomnia. . . .

The United States is a country where everything must be paid for, with two honorable exceptions: the ice vomited up by machines strategically placed in hotels and service stations, and matches, which are publicity tools offered by cigarette machines and free at any hotel or restaurant of any category. However, there is an institutionalized payment that surprises me: the tip. It is a quasi-imposition that I consider contradictory in a society like the United States. In fact, the philosophy that informs American life is one of merit, of success, and of justice.

It seems to me that in this society, to give a tip would be to humiliate someone who fulfills his or her duty, renders a service, or performs a task that does not need to be rewarded beyond the normal circuit. Tips pay favors, compensate insufficiencies and not duties, and are the embryo of corruption. They never will be just, even in societies where class differences are clandestine or hidden. Tips in the States are equivocal; they are a form of oblivion and in contradiction to American life and values.

A big country, from a geographical point of view, the United States is a country closed in on itself. Americans know little about the world, except when a plane crashes in Germany, a revolution takes place in Portugal (located about seven hours away by air), or when the king of Spain dies. On the other hand, we always know when an American president has a toothache, when a Hollywood star gets divorced for the third time, or when there is a rally for legalizing marijuana. This focus can be understood by the fact that the United States is a country at an intercontinental level, with several dozen states that function almost like European countries. Isn't it true that a middle-class American will spend his or her vacation in another American state? This virtual autism derives from another important factor within American daily life—the television. The American TV, a complex and overwhelming hydra, reports live on car accidents at the street corner, interviews the storekeeper on our block, or covers the "League of Friends" of something or another. The only international issues reported, in fact, are those directly related to the United States of America. Besides these, only natural disasters, revolutions, and air accidents are covered. The world is too far away: Europe is too distant, South America is not very close either, and only the immediate geographical space is subject to attention. TV imperialism and the enormous publicity machine suffer from umbilical narcissism, exploitable at any moment.

The American family is an enigmatic institution, both protective and uncaring. When I reflect on the concept of family, the transmission of values, and the conveying of parental authority, which is simultaneously rigid and relaxed, I feel that something is wrong; that is, there is something essentially different from these concepts in Europe. I admit my bias and some ethnocentrism, but I question the attitudes of American youth. For example, the obsession for alcoholic drinks when one reaches the authorized or legal age (which varies from state to state) appears to be in contradiction with family values conveyed to youngsters. I had many opportunities to observe young people, boys and girls, who used to get drunk, mixing various types of alcoholic drinks. When I asked several groups the reason for such mixtures, the answer was always the same: "We mix the drinks in order to get drunk as soon as possible." It is true that not all American youths proceed in this manner, but it is also true that the great ambition of a youngster eighteen years of age is to leave his or her parents' home. The wish for autonomy and freedom, and the obsessive thirst for alcoholic drinks, seem too radical and are a strange rupture within family tutorship. That is the reason I suggest that something is not going well in the family educational system in the United States. I hope to be forgiven by those who think I am generalizing too readily.

During my first visits to America, I thought there was a kind of empty space in relation to social control. I thought in these terms because I was a foreigner and apparently anonymous. In fact, in this respect American society is not so different from others. In large urban centers, naturally, interpersonal relations are marked by a great indifference, but that happens all around the world. By the same token, in American rural areas, as in rural areas worldwide, there are forms of social control, more or less visible, more or less subtle. What happens to the foreign visitor and observer is the initial blindness in the face of novelty and the unknown. Such blindness does not allow us to focus our dispersed attention on the analysis of social phenomena in their real proportions and profundity.

My son Carlos went to Los Angeles to spend a vacation. It was agreed that he would stay one and a half months in the house of our friends. Before his departure, I gave him some advice and information about the American way of life. During his stay he used to call me, but the tone of his voice did not sound very convincing when he informed me that he was truly enjoying his "American dream." After twenty-nine days, I received an unexpected phone call:

"Father, meet me at the airport, I'm coming back tomorrow!"
"But why so early?"
"I'll tell you later."

The next day, I went to the Lisbon airport. As soon as he saw me he gave me a hug and sighed,

"I wanted so much to return, but I already regret having come!"

That's exactly what America provokes in us: an ambivalent sentiment of love and rejection, in a type of overwhelming anguish that generates the ambition to go to America and the wish to come back quickly.

My son's thirty days in America were a unique experience that is a dream for many Portuguese and European youngsters of his age and that had also been the unreachable ambition of my own youth. Carlos wants to return to the States, and nowadays he is showing his intercontinental behavior with the consumption of many liters of Pepsi or Coca Cola and enormous portions of ketchup, popcorn, and French-fried potatoes.

Meanwhile, I notice that he makes a show of using slang phrases that he has taken to his English classes. Naturally, this has not helped him earn good grades.

Since Carlos returned, he systematically uses coded expressions. He now says, "It's really good over there; there things are better; when I was there . . . ; there I could heat my orange juice in the microwave; there we can find everything." After some time, it was easy for me to conclude that for my son *there* means America.

A Portuguese of middle-class background can usually speak several languages. This situation is much appreciated by Americans, and we are normally well respected given our capacity to communicate in three or four languages: our mother tongue, English, French, and Spanish or German. For us, this was always a necessary or a natural thing: Besides our own language, it is not difficult for us to speak in Spanish; we have a long and great tradition connected with French culture and the French language; and in order to understand Americans, we need to speak English. Americans find themselves in an inferior position because neither history nor necessity has forced them to learn other languages. For some Americans, the ability to speak French is an indicator of incomparable prestige. I think that some Americans insist on enriching their vocabulary with French words and expressions, even if they cannot speak the language fluently. The Portuguese visitor wins some status and security given his or her role as a polyglot. However, in other situations, the Portuguese visitor gapes at the spectacular achievements (in terms of material culture and social pragmatism) of so-called American civilization.

We are amazed, for example, that the prestige of certain professions in America is not as low as is the case in Portugal. I think, in contrast, that Americans grant more dignity to the worker, regardless of the type of job performed. In the United States, a farmer, a taxi driver, or a traveling salesperson would not necessarily feel inferior; in Portugal, however, these are truly minor professions. In Portugal, too, an economist, an anthropologist, or a graduate in chemistry would almost never perform the aforementioned "lowly" jobs. "It does not become one" and "it looks bad" would be the first justifications.

In fact, this problem is linked either to the labor market or to the educational system, to access to the university, and to the total proportions of graduates, which are quite different both in quality and quantity in these countries.

The United States values community associations in a way we think exemplary. Cooperative projects, professional and sectorial associations, defense leagues, and friends groups proliferate in the heart of American society. In a land that has recently fomented excessive narcissism and individualism, it is interesting to note the conciliation of these two philosophies and postures.

Indeed, in the end, I know extremely little about the United States of America. Probably, my American glasses have given me a blurred, out-of-focus image of reality.

The posture of a Portuguese can be ridiculous when in America. I remember that my son warmed his orange juice in the microwave to soothe his sore throat. Our difficulty in determining on which side a door opens is ridiculous. We Portuguese do not take showers after meals, we think it dangerous for our health to eat oranges at night, we make a lot of noise when we blow our noses, we rarely go to bed before midnight, and we spend enormous amounts of time at the table.

Any American, in turn, would grin at this strange behavior.

REFERENCES

LINTON, RALPH
1936   The Study of Man. Madison, WI: D. Appleton-Century.
1937   One Hundred Percent American. American Mercury 40:427–429.

MINER, HORACE
1956   Body Ritual Among the Nacirema. American Anthropologist 58:503–507.

SANTOS, JOSÉ
1989   Entrevista a Octávio Paz. Lisboa: Semanário (Setembro).

⊜ American Graffiti: Curious Derivatives of Individualism

JIN K. KIM
State University of New York, Plattsburgh

Professor Kim is visited by his closest high school friend, whom he has not seen for twenty years. During his visit, his friend, who hopes to immigrate to the United States, calls Kim an "American." In response and in order to aid his friend's transition to life in "this land of dreams," Kim writes him a letter. From a Korean cultural perspective, American issues of privacy, manners, sexual mores, individuality, interpersonal relations, and doublespeak are forthrightly and entertainingly addressed.

Jin K. Kim, *born and raised in South Korea, completed a B.A. degree in English at Sogang Jesuit University, Seoul, and came to the United States in 1972, where he pursued graduate study in communication at Syracuse University and the University of Iowa (Ph.D., 1978). Currently Kim is an associate professor in the Department of Communication, SUNY Plattsburgh. His teaching and scholarly interests include intercultural communication, communication theory, and mass communication law.*

Dear MK,

I sincerely hope the last leg of your trip home from the five-week fact-finding visit to the United States was pleasant and informative. Although I may not have expressed my sense of exhilaration about your visit through the meager lodging accommodations and "barbaric" foods we provided, it was sheer joy to spend four weeks with you and Kyung-Ok. (Please refrain from hitting the ceiling. My use of your charming wife's name, rather than the usual Korean expression, "your wife" or "your house person," is not an indication of my amorous intentions toward her as any red-blooded Korean man would suspect. Since you are planning to immigrate to this country soon, I thought you might as well begin to get used to the idea of your wife exerting her individuality. Better yet, I thought you should be warned that the moment the plane touches American soil, you will lose your status as the center of your familial universe.) At any rate, please be assured that during your stay here my heart was filled with memories of our three years together in high school when we were young in Pusan. It was indeed thirty years ago when we were as mischievous and curiosity-driven as any youngsters can be. Since then, your worst fear, formed on the basis of my indefatigable appetite for books, has come true: "All you could achieve in your life is to become a stuffy scholar." In the meantime, riding smoothly on the rising tide of Korea as an economic power, you have amassed a small fortune, which you want to use as a down payment for an even bigger fortune in this land of dreams. Honestly, MK, an immigrant with a multi-million dollar bank account is quite incongruent with the images of those millions who came to this country in response to the invitation: "Send me your poor, your tired, your huddled masses yearning to be free. . . ." But then, the world has changed, especially in the past twenty years when we were separated from each other. If we could revive our friendship after all these years, if my twenty-year experience as an "alien" can contribute even one iota to making you less an "alien" in this country, and if your wealth can be justifiably used to the benefit of a new generation of the poor, tired, and huddled masses of present economic hardships in my adopted fatherland, I will gladly sell my soul and volunteer to you every bit of my personal "wisdom" on what America is about. It is true that the peculiar pattern of life I have lived in the last two decades is likely to have tainted that "wisdom." But then, my old friend, do you know any wisdom that transcends its experiential boundaries?

During your visit, you called me, on several occasions, an American. What prompted you to invoke such a reference is beyond my comprehension. Was it my rusty Korean expressions? Was it my calculating mind? Was it my pitifully subservient (at least when viewed through your cultural lens) role that I was playing in the family life? Or, was it my familiarity with some facets of the American cultural landscape? This may sound bewildering to you, but it is absolutely true that through all the years I have lived in this country, I never truly felt like an American. Sure, on the surface, our family followed closely many ritualistic routines of the American culture: shopping malls, vacations, dining out, holidays, weddings, funerals, summer camps, PTA volunteer works, community service, Little League baseball games, concerts, plays, movies, community youth orchestras, museums, art galleries, picnics, birthday parties, camping trips, Wrigley Field, state fairs, county fairs, jazz festivals, food carnivals, casinos, amusement parks, beaches, National Parks, fast-food chains, credit card shopping sprees, Nintendo games, board games, game shows, situation comedies, soap operas, hot dogs, apple pies (no Chevrolet yet), fund-raising dinners, retirement parties, church potlucks, the health food craze, fitness programs, Tupperware parties, and, of course, Amway fantasies. I always considered my participation in these "rituals" as none other than the act of a half-hearted spectator who was being pushed by circumstances. My physical involvement in these activities was undeniable, but mentally I remained stubbornly in the periphery. Naturally, then, my subjective cultural attitudes stayed staunchly Korean. Never did the inner layers of my Korean psyche yield to the invading American cultural vagaries, I thought. Of course, I would not rule out the possibility of the outer layers being coated here and there with an American frame of reference. My subjective feeling about my cultural identity notwithstanding, when you labeled me an American for the first time, I felt a twinge of guilt.

Several years ago, an old Korean friend of mine, who settled in the United States about the same time I did, paid a visit to Korea for the first time in some fifteen years. When he went to see his best high school friend, who was now married and had two sons, his friend's wife made a bed for him and her husband in the master bedroom, declaring that she would spend the night with the children. It was not necessarily the sexual connotation of the episode that made my friend blush; he was greatly embarrassed by the circumstance in which he imposed himself to the extent that the couple's privacy had to be violated. For his high school friend and his wife, it was clearly their age-old friendship to which the couple's privacy had to yield. MK, you might empathize rather easily with this Korean couple's state of mind. But it would be a gross mistake even to imagine there may be occasions in your adopted culture when a gesture of friendship breaks the barrier of privacy. Zealously guarding their privacy above all, Americans are marvelously adept at drawing the line where friendship—that elusive "we" feeling—stops and privacy begins.

My first Greyhound bus trip in 1972 was a long one from Milwaukee, Wisconsin, to Syracuse, New York. During this twenty-four-hour trip, I met a divorced Catholic woman who confided in me the most intimate aspects of her private life, including her sexual hang-ups. By the time I got off the bus, she not only gave me her telephone number but also demanded I call her daughter who was allegedly a student at Syracuse University. Two weeks after this incident, I rushed to Massachusetts to visit Michelle and Bob. You may remember these Americans whom I befriended at college in Korea; they had come to our university, in the midst of the Vietnam War, to do "peace" work instead of being involved in the acts of savagery in the Southeast Asian rice paddies. Our friendship, conceived and nurtured in the homespun Korean cultural climate, was indeed a special one. I ran, never without enthusiasm, the extra mile to make their life in a strange land comfortable and trouble free. They were equally intrigued with the intensely personal nature of the cross-cultural experiences I was providing for them. Our mutual respect and affection were such that Bob and I even showed unmanly tears at the airport when they returned to the States after three years. You can imagine, MK, how heartbroken I was when I arrived in that small New England city and was told they had been separated for several months. Their Korean-born son, Daniel, was on a biweekly parental-visit schedule. I had to ape Daniel's visiting schedule, seeing my old friends separately. On the second night I spent with Bob, he had a small dinner party for several of his friends, and I met an interesting woman with a radical political viewpoint. She was apparently a hard-core Maoist with a strong conviction that only a Mao-style revolution could solve America's mounting problems of the time. After dinner, she cordially invited me—me alone, that is—to her apartment, which was in the same building as Bob's. When I knocked on her door fifteen minutes later, I was greeted with a lifesize poster of Chairman Mao hanging on the living room wall. (Remember, MK, this was in 1972 when I was in this country on a student visa. If the Korean CIA agents or their informants, who were known to be closely monitoring activities of Korean students in the United States, were tipped off about my "association" with a Maoist, I could easily have been blacklisted.) That gigantic red poster alone was sufficient to make my heart palpitate, but, my friend, it was nothing compared to what I was to discover next. On a more careful scrutiny of the woman with whom I found myself alone, I realized she was in a see-through evening dress with nothing under it! Admittedly, it was a hot summer evening, and even a most stoic Confucian disciple might have chosen relaxing attire. Even so, displaying the most private parts of her body to a virtual stranger completely threw me off. To be honest with you, I have no recollection of how coherent I was that night when I argued against the inhuman nature of Communist ideology, especially as it was practiced in the Chinese Communist Revolution, which claimed approximately eight million human lives.

These two encounters—that is, the one with the babbling woman on the Greyhound bus and the other with the naked Maoist revolution-ary—led me to believe, however temporarily, that in America a volun-tary abandonment of one's privacy precedes a long-lasting personal friendship. In Korea, as I remember, MK, it was always a lengthy friend-ship that was used as a pretext to forgo one's own privacy or violate that of another person.

Several days later, it was time to visit Michelle and her son. After spend-ing a splendid New England summer afternoon on a beach where Michelle painfully explained how her separation from Bob came about, we headed home in her brand new Volvo. Out of curiosity and anxiety about my transportation problem in Syracuse, I asked Michelle, "How much did you pay for this car?"

"Michael, you do not ask a question like that in the States," said she, using my baptismal name.

"What do you mean?" I responded, perplexed.

"Because it is a matter of privacy. If you really need to know, 'Did you get a good deal for this car?' would be more appropriate," Michelle stated matter-of-factly.

As her voice or look did not indicate any sign that she was less than serious, I repressed my urge to protest against her apparent contradiction. What about our six-year friendship, I thought, and all the intimate facts of private life involving the imminent divorce, which she just passed on to me at the beach? My perplexity and puzzlement were slow to diminish, since she never told me how much she paid for the car.

Indeed, one of the hardest tasks you will face as an "alien" is how to find that delicate balance between your individuality (for example, privacy) and your collective identity (for example, friendship or membership in social groups). Privacy is not the only issue that stems from this individuality-collectivity continuum. Honesty in interpersonal relationships is another point that may keep you puzzled. Americans are almost brutally honest and frank about issues that belong to public domains; they are not afraid of discussing an embarrassing topic in most graphic details as long as the topic is a matter of public concern. Equally frank and honest gestures are adopted when they discuss their own personal lives once the presumed benefits from such gestures are determined to outweigh the risks involved. Accordingly, it is not uncommon to encounter friends who volunteer personally embarrassing and even shameful information lest you find it out from other sources. Are Americans equally straightforward and forthcoming in laying out heartfelt personal criticisms directed at their friends? Not likely. Their otherwise acute sense of honesty becomes significantly muted when they face the unpleasant task of being negative toward their personal friends. The fear of an emotion-draining confrontation and the virtue of being polite force them to put on a facade or mask. The perfectly accepted social behavior of telling "white lies" is a good example. The social and personal virtues of accepting such lies are grounded in the belief that the potential damage that can be inflicted by directly telling a friend the hurtful truth far outweighs the potential benefit that the friend could gain from it. Instead of telling a hurtful truth directly, Americans use various indirect communication channels to which their friend is likely to be tuned. In other words, they publicize the information in the form of gossip or behind-the-back recriminations until it is transformed into a sort of collective criticism against the target individual. Thus objectified and collectivized, the "truth" ultimately reaches the target individual with a minimal cost of social discomfort on the part of the teller. There is nothing vile or insidious about this communication tactic, since it is deeply rooted in the concern for sustaining social pleasantry for both parties.

This innocuous practice, however, is bound to be perceived as an act of outrageous dishonesty by a person deeply immersed in the Korean culture. In the Korean cultural context, a trusted personal relationship precludes such publicizing prior to direct, "honest" criticism to the individual concerned, no matter what the cost in social and personal unpleasantry. Indeed, as you are well aware, MK, such direct reproach and even recrimination in Korea is in most cases appreciated as a sign of one's utmost love and concern for the target individual. Stressful and emotionally draining as it is, such a frank expression of criticism is done out of "we" feeling. Straight-talking friends did not want me to repeat undesirable acts in front of others, as it would either damage "our reputation" or go against the common interest of "our collective identity." In Korea, the focus is on the self-discipline that forms a basis for the integrity of "our group." In America, on the other hand, the focus is on the feelings of two individuals. From the potential teller's viewpoint, the primary concern is how to maintain social politeness, whereas from the target person's viewpoint, the primary concern is how to maintain self-esteem. Indeed, these two diametrically opposed frames of reference—self-discipline and self-esteem—make one culture collective and the other individualistic. It is rather amazing that for all the mistakes I must have made in the past twenty years, only one non-Korean American friend gave me such an "honest" criticism. In a sense, this concern for interpersonal politeness conceals their disapproval of my undesirable behavior for a time and ultimately delays the adjustment or realignment of my behavior, since it is likely to take quite a while for the collective judgment to reach me through the "publicized" channels of communication. So many Korean immigrants express their indignation about their American colleagues who smile at them but who criticize them behind their backs. If you ever become a victim of such a perception, MK, please take heart that you are not the only one who feels that pain.

At a societal level, too, the American tendency to close their eyes in an effort to avoid unpleasant realities surfaces in the form of a widespread use of euphemisms, especially in public life. Deaf people, for instance, become "hearing impaired." Proponents of abortion lace the dark reality of the actual acts with a glittering catch phrase, "pro-choice," while their antagonists, some of whom do not mind throwing bombs into abortion clinics, describe themselves as "pro-lifers." Americans take comfort at the rhetorical cosmetic surgery of calling housewives "domestic engineers." A simple tax raise transforms into "revenue enhancement," and American paratroopers invading another nation is called "a predawn vertical insertion." A hospital where an anesthetist kills a mother and her unborn child with an accidental overdose of nitrous oxide calls the deaths a "therapeutic misadventure." When potato chip delivery truck drivers are described in a "help wanted" ad as "executive snack route consultants," you realize how serious this epidemic is.

In a sense, Americans' reluctance and evasiveness in confronting unpleasant realities represent an inconsistent application of the meaning of individualism to a variety of human behaviors. The fundamental belief in the value and free will of individuals in pursuing the greatest good to the greatest number with minimal interference from state or societal constraints is vigorously advocated and even glorified when individual efforts bear fruit. Thus, when a rugged individual successfully overcomes adverse social and economic conditions, Americans elevate the man or woman to the status of hero for his or her spirit of independence. The individual is praised for fighting against the encroachment of collective forces. The individual is also likely to claim the well-deserved credit for achieving that status. However, when things go wrong, when those individuals fail to achieve what they set out to achieve, or when they become victims of circumstances, the same individualistic mentality takes a 180-degree turn; no individual accepts the responsibility or blame for the failure or admits the mishap was a reasonable consequence of risk taking in the normal course of life. Fearful of the immense cost of admitting one's failure, Americans too readily blame others for all sorts of things—from inadequate educational achievements (for example, "The school failed to teach me how to read" or "SAT questions are gender/race-biased") to murder (for example, "I plead not guilty by reason of insanity") to alcoholism (for example, "I inherited alcoholic genes"). The expression "I am sorry" comes out naturally from the mouths of Americans, as you will find out soon, MK. By no means do they use the expression indiscriminately, however. That apologetic statement is made mostly when the consequence of that gesture remains absolutely negligible. When matters of substance or legal responsibilities are involved, it would be virtually impossible to hear that statement. Admission of individual faults is such a precious commodity in the American cultural landscape! (As you will realize after your life as an immigrant progresses to an advanced stage, this reluctance in admitting fault also has to do with the prevalent role that litigation plays in American life.) More frequently than not, you are likely to wonder, "Where does the unwavering faith in individual spirit fade away to when problems arise?"

It was the summer of 1963 when you and I spent a month at a Buddhist temple preparing for the "Gate of Hell" (college entrance exam). Do you still remember our meeting with that Bee-goo-nee [unmarried female monk] who was "repenting" for her "sin"? Before she settled in the deadly silence of the Buddhist temple, she had passed a bar exam as the first female to do so in Korea and had become a trial judge. Her fate was such that she sentenced a murder suspect to death, but after the prisoner was executed, the real murderer was arrested. Tormented by the guilt and existential limitation of human reasoning, she, at the age of twenty-seven, changed her black judge's robe for a shabby gray monk's robe and cut off her connections to the secular world. At the time we faced her saddened eyes, she was approaching her sixties. "Thirty years of personal penitence for a collective error of the legal system? Was she insane?" I remember asking myself repeatedly.

Since then, however, MK, her eyes with those indelible marks of suffering have bothered me on innumerable occasions when I had to attribute my failure to external conditions. When my car was towed away from the no-parking stretch of that Montreal street near the Botanical Garden where you and I visited during your stay here, you personally witnessed my furious response. Unfortunately, I have no way of recollecting whether that was one of the times you called me an American.

MK—

The last facet of the individualism-collectivism continuum likely to cause a great amount of cognitive dissonance in the process of your assimilation to American life is the extent to which you have to assert your individuality to other people. You probably have no difficulty remembering our high school principal, K. W. Park, for whom we had a respect-contempt complex. He used to lecture, almost daily at morning assemblies, on the virtue of being modest. As he preached it, it was a form of the Confucian virtue of self-denial. Our existence or presence among other people, he told us, should not be overly felt through communicated messages (regardless of whether they are done with a tongue or pen). His most frequently quoted verse from Lao-tzu's *Tao Te Ching* was:

> True words aren't eloquent;
>   eloquent words aren't true.
> Wise men don't need to prove their point;
>   men who need to prove their point aren't wise.
>
> The Master has no possessions.
> The more he does for others,
>   the happier he is.
> The more he gives to others,
>   the wealthier he is.
>
> The Tao nourishes by not forcing.
> By not dominating, the Master leads.

The Taoist principal, Park, was a fervent advocate of "conspicuous subtletly" in presenting oneself. He was not subtle at all about instilling in our budding minds his "messianic" message that self-advertisement was the worst form to let others know about "my existence." One's existence, we were told, should be noticed by others in the form of our acts and conduct. One is obligated to provide opportunities for others to experience one's existence through what he or she does. Self-initiated effort for public recognition or self-aggrandizement was the most shameful conduct for a person of virtue.

This idea is interesting and noble as a philosophical posture, but when it is practiced in America, it will not get you anywhere in most circumstances. The lack of self-assertion is translated directly into timidity and lack of self-confidence. This is a culture where you must exert your individuality to the extent that it would make our high school principal turn in his grave out of shame and disgust. Blame the size of the territory or the population of this country. You may even blame the fast-paced cadence of life or the social mobility that moves people around at a dizzying speed. Whatever the specific reason might be, Americans are not waiting to experience you or your behaviors as they exist. They want a "documented" version of you that is eloquently summarized, decorated, and certified. What they are looking for is not your raw, unprocessed being with rich texture; rather, it is a slickly processed self, neatly packaged and, most important, conveniently delivered to them. Self-advertising is encouraged almost to the point of pretentiousness. Years ago in Syracuse, I had an occasion to introduce a visiting Korean monk-scholar to a gathering of people who wanted to hear something about Oriental philosophies. After taking an elegantly practiced bow to the crowd, this humble monk declared, "My name is . . . Please teach me, as I do not know anything." It took quite a bit of probing and questioning for us to extract something to chew on from that monk with the mysterious smile. Contrast this with an American colleague of mine applying for a promotion several years ago, who literally hauled in two cabinets full of documented evidence of his scholarly achievements.

MK—
I am afraid this rambling letter really bored you with inconsequential topics, which might not have any bearing on your immigrant's life as a businessman. Seriously, however, if your business is such that you are dependent (both literally and figuratively) on Korean ethnic institutions in large cities such as Los Angeles, New York, or Chicago, none of these derivatives of the individualism-collectivism continuum may pose any threat or hindrance to your career. The "institutional completeness" of a contemporary immigrant society is so thorough that an immigrant who chooses to do so can lead a relatively undisturbed life thickly insulated from the mainstream. Because of a tremendous improvement in communication technologies and transportation, an immigrant living in a heavily ethnic environment—especially an immigrant from a country like Korea where the nation's communications infrastructure was developed in an American mold—maintains virtually the same information environment as the one in the original homeland. Daily satellite feeds of TV news programs, instant satellite transmission and subsequent reprinting of the newspapers from the homeland, videotapes of the popular TV dramas airlifted within one or two days after the original broadcasts, and the constant infusion of visitors from home all conjure to create a cultural climate radically different from the one that many earlier immigrants faced—a forced acculturation. It is becoming an increasing reality—a very tempting one indeed—to live in America without really leaving "home." Should such a home-away-from-home life-style

become your choice, more than likely what I have scribbled here will not mean much for your immediate future as a businessman. But then, I may ask, what about your children when they start bringing home the debris of friction with the mainstream culture? The curious journey toward the American end of the individualism-collectivism continuum will be inevitable, I assure you. The real question is whether it will be in your generation, your children's, or their children's. Whenever it happens, it will be a bittersweet revenge for me, since only then will you realize how it feels to be called an American by your best high school chum.

SUGGESTED READINGS

HYUN, PETER
1984   Koreana. Seoul, Korea: Korea Britannica Corporation.

LIU, ZONGREN
1988   Two Years in the Melting Pot. San Francisco: China Books and Periodicals.

LUTZ, WILLIAM
1989   Double Speak. New York: Harper & Row.

MITCHELL, STEPHEN
1988   Tao Te Ching. New York: Harper & Row.

MOORE, BARRINGTON, JR.
1984   Privacy: Studies in Social and Cultural History. Armonk, NY: M. E. Sharpe.

YOSHIKAWA, MUNEO JAY
1988   Cross-Cultural Adaptation and Perceptual Development. In Cross-Cultural Adaptation: Current Approaches. Young Y. Kim and William B. Gudykunst, eds. Newbury Park, CA: Sage.

THREE

An Outsider's View of American Culture

JANUSZ L. MUCHA
Nicolaus Copernicus University, Torun, Poland

A frequent visitor to America, Professor Mucha compares his European idea of the "city" to what he discovered in the United States. The immediate and informal cordiality of Americans is also discussed, as is urban anonymity, the profane naturalness of violence, patriotism, education, ethnocentrism, and the American potluck dinner.

Janusz L. Mucha *is professor of Sociology at Nicolaus Copernicus University, in Torun, Poland. He received an M.A. in Sociology, an M.A. in Philosophy, a Ph.D. in Humanities, and a Habilitation Degree from the Jagiellonian University of Cracow, Poland. He also studied as a postdoctoral fellow at the Johns Hopkins University; the Bologna Center in Italy; the Taras Shevchenko University in Kiev, Ukraine; the University of Wisconsin; and the University of Chicago. His primary fields of interest are urban communities of Native Americans and Polish-Americans and the symbolic anthropology of Polish society.*

It is quite difficult to look at American culture with a fresh eye. One can easily become bewildered or upset, especially if one comes from a country where America has been treated as something special. And, in my case, having an education based on American sociology, cultural anthropology, and social psychology, having read all the classics of American literature, and having watched many movies, both classic and modern, directed by both foreigners and Americans, confusion about the culture persists. Further, this being my fifth time in the United States, having lived for months in big cities like Chicago and New York, in small towns like Stevens Point, Wisconsin, and South Bend, Indiana, I have had an opportunity to view, firsthand, the diversity of American culture.

Having the experience mentioned, liking America, and being rather flexible, I see how one can easily lose the sense of novelty of first contact and view this initial contact through later experiences. Ultimately, one too easily begins to treat everything as normal; one attempts to understand everything, perceive the causes of everything that is going on, and frame one's observations and experiences into some structural and functional context.

Nothing bewilders or upsets me in America. After all these years I still see things that are different here than they are in both my native Poland and the many other countries that I have visited. Unfortunately, these observations are neither novel nor original: They are, or at least should be, obvious to many people, foreigners and Americans alike.

I love nature, but I am a city boy. I was born and raised and had lived for forty years in Cracow, a medieval university town of a half million inhabitants in southern Poland. An urban environment is very important to me. This is something I miss in America. The idea of the "city," as I conceive it, hardly exists in America. My idea of "city" can be found in parts of three American cities: San Francisco, New York, and New Orleans. There is a noticeable lack of an urban environment in America. I do not refer here to the fact of the deserted, burned-out, or depopulated parts of cities. I have noticed many empty, run-down apartment houses that would be put to good use in Poland. What I refer to is the physical and social structure of the towns and cities of America. It is the exception in America to have the excellent public transportation found in Vienna, Paris, London, and even Warsaw. In many American cities there are not even sidewalks: The people rarely walk, so why invest in sidewalks? If one jogs, one can use the street or roadway. American drivers understand the use of the roads for exercise and, unless a driver is drunk, there's not much risk.

Not only are there no sidewalks, there are no squares where people can safely gather, meet other people, talk, or buy flowers. There are no coffee shops like in Vienna, Rome, or Budapest. If you want coffee, you must drive to McDonald's or go to a restaurant. If you walk beyond the environs of "downtown," or the shopping mall, you will most likely be stopped by a police officer who will, if you are white, offer to assist you. But how can the officer be of assistance? Can he or she give you a ride to a real cafe? Can he or she return you to the "downtown" that, after dark, is most often both unsafe and deserted? There is no such thing as a real theater, and the movie theaters are back at the shopping mall, far removed from the empty downtowns of America.

Numerous sociologists and cultural anthropologists tend to identify American urban life with anonymity, the lack of primary groups and face-to-face contact, with only superficial and formal relationships. How do I see America? I have experienced a lot of friendliness and kindness in America. Everyone wants to help me, to thank me for calling or for stopping by. Everyone seems to care about me. When I make new acquaintances, including the dental hygienist, everyone addresses me by my first name, and I can be certain that he or she will make every effort to pronounce it as correctly as possible. Very soon, I discover that I am learning many intimate details of the personal lives of the people I have just met. I find myself a bit embarrassed, but I doubt that they are. They become my friends so quickly, and as quickly they begin to share their problems with me. There are, in the English language, the nouns *colleague,* and *acquaintance,* but I do not discover them to be in popular use. In America, when one meets someone, he or she immediately becomes a *friend.* Does this mean, for instance, that you can expect to be invited to his or her home for dinner or to just sit and talk? Absolutely not. I have often been invited to dinner, but perhaps I have been fortunate in meeting a different type of American. My brother, who teaches Russian and Polish at a Texas university, had not been invited to anyone's house for dinner during the entire academic year. My American friend, who teaches history in a New England college, had not been invited to anyone's home during her first year in the small college town. Therefore, I am forced to conclude that quality friendships in the sense of lasting, intimate, emotionally involving relationships are more difficult to develop.

In reference to the anonymity of urban life, as I have mentioned earlier, urban "life" hardly exists. There are neighborhoods, however, and "urban villagers" reside therein. Is this anonymity a feature of these neighborhoods? I do know, at least by the faces, everyone who lives in my own neighborhood in South Bend. If I do not recognize someone, I can tell whether that person "belongs" to my neighborhood. If a nonresident is in the neighborhood, he or she will be singled out immediately. It is possible that a patrol car will stop and a police officer will kindly ask the stranger to produce identification. A black person obviously cannot rely on anonymity in a predominantly white neighborhood. Neighborhoods do not want anonymity. The neighbors, in this instance, want to know everyone, to be able to address everyone by his or her first name, to be able to say "hello," and to ask how one is doing. And, as I've learned, they prefer the answer to be brief and positive: "I am fine, thank you."

An obvious reason for this fear of urban anonymity is the problem of security. However, the lack of anonymity does not imply that the relationships are truly friendly in the deeper sense of the word. The neighbors know each other, but they do not visit each other's homes to sit and talk, to exchange recipes, to borrow household tools, or to help if the automobile is not running. In this age of telephones, neighbors do not ordinarily just stop by unexpectedly.

American society is famous for the brutality of social life. The high rate of violent crime is incomprehensible. Rapes, female battering, child abuse, and molestation are the lead stories for local television and the print media. This information about violence has many positive consequences. If we wish to fight something, if we want to prevent crime, we must be aware of it. However, the constant forced awareness—the information on why and how someone was killed or raped—accustoms Americans to violence. They treat it as something natural, as just another case of a person killing or being killed. Violent death or abuse belongs to the profane, ordinary world of America. There is nothing sacred about it, unless it is the residual fear that it can also happen to you. On the other hand, death of natural causes is almost completely removed from everyday lives. Old people die in nursing homes or hospitals, and even this type of death, in being generally ignored, does not belong to the sphere of the sacred.

The fact of violence in everyday American life has numerous social consequences. One consequence is the decline of urban life. Americans have now accepted the fact that downtown areas, after dark, belong to the criminals or misfits. Americans accept the fact that strangers may be dangerous. Americans, thus, try to avoid downtown areas and strangers, especially at night.

Patriotism is another feature of American life that appears to differ from many European countries. I have been exposed to patriotism for the greatest part of my life. However, Polish patriotism, or nationalism, is different. Poland was, for forty-five years, under Communist rule, which was, to some extent, accepted, although the majority of Polish society treated it as alien domination. The Communists monopolized the use of national symbols. In the mid-1970s, the ruling party made it illegal to use these symbols without special permission by the state authorities. I can recall the unauthorized use of national symbols only within the religious context. I have never seen a Polish national flag in a private residence. Only once in my life did I see an eagle, the Polish national symbol, in a private residence. From my interpretation, the old national symbols became identified with a state that was not treated as the true embodiment of the national institutions. In America, state and nation are symbolically identified, and, moreover, nearly everyone feels the necessity to emphasize his or her identification with nation or state. I will not elaborate on the yellow ribbons in evidence during the Persian Gulf War, but it seems to me necessary to mention the presence of the American flag in most residences, offices, and clubs I have visited. Further, Lions Club lunches, university graduations, basketball games, and so on all begin with the singing of the national anthem.

Is there anything wrong with these public displays of patriotism? I do not believe so. However, the use of national symbols on an everyday basis has, in my opinion, two questionable consequences. First, the meanings of these symbols are shifting from the sacred to the profane, ordinary, everyday sphere of life. Second, the public display may indicate a strong degree of ethnocentrism. Excessive patriotism, pride in country and its achievements, may signify—and I am convinced that this is true in America—a very strong and blinding conviction that the American ways are much better than the ways of other countries and peoples. After all these years, after all these arrivals and departures, and after all these meetings with many Americans in Poland and in other countries of Europe, my impression is that American people, especially as visitors to foreign areas, are friendly but arrogant. They are arrogant in the sense that they do not understand non-American customs and habits, they do not even try to understand, and they are convinced that other customs "must" be much worse simply because they are not American. Americans are friendly in the sense that they would sympathize with other people; they would pity them and give them advice on how they should elevate themselves . . . to become more American.

What are the reasons for this general behavior and attitude? One reason is that the American educational system does not promote general knowledge about the United States and other countries. Personally, I am not of the opinion that education is the best solution to *all* social problems. Moreover, I believe that the significance of education is often exaggerated by politicians and mass media. However, American students at the grade school, middle school, and high school levels do know *much* less than students their ages outside of the United States. How can students learn more if no one demands that they learn more? I used to participate in monthly faculty meetings of the College of Liberal Arts and Sciences at a state university. Each month, a part of the agenda was a discussion of the admission policy. Should we accept candidates who cannot read, write, and calculate? Eventually, we continued to accept these deficient students . . . to a university! Their knowledge of their own country is minimal and inadequate. Their knowledge of other parts of the world is practically nonexistent. This may be the foundation for Americans' deep convictions that their ways are superior. They know little of their own country and less about other countries. What little they know is evidently the basis for their unquestioned views.

Another reason for the "friendly arrogance" of Americans may be their relative parochialism. The United States is so large and diverse that it is very difficult to learn much more than something of one's own state and, perhaps, neighboring states. Geographically and culturally (regions, ethnic groups), the United States is indeed so diverse that one can travel and study it for years, always learning something new and interesting. But, from my point of view of the whole of humankind, this big and diverse nation is only one relatively homogeneous spot on a map, a spot in which nearly everyone speaks the same language, can stay at the same type of hotel or motel, eat in the same type of restaurant, and shop at the same kind of supermarket. People living in Europe have a much better opportunity to appreciate the world's cultural diversity and to become much more relativistic than Americans. Europe remains a continent of natural cultural diversity, and the differences in the European educational system help in developing a relativistic attitude toward other peoples and customs. Naturally, not all Europeans take advantage of their educational opportunities, and they too often remain as rigidly ethnocentric as many educated Americans.

A third reason why the American is generally more ethnocentric than the average European is the nature of mass media. Reading American dailies (with perhaps the exception of the *New York Times, Chicago Tribune, Washington Post, USA Today,* and a few others), we get an impression that the entire world consists of some extension of the United States. In weekday editions, we rarely learn of the world beyond the Atlantic and Pacific Oceans, or even north and south of the nation's borders. In the case of an assassination of a public figure, a revolution, a minor war, or a significant natural catastrophe, we may learn something of the world beyond the borders. On a regular basis, we learn very little of other countries. I have discovered that educated people are not certain if Poles use the Latin or Cyrillic alphabet, if the Polish language is distinct from Russian, or if the Poles had their own army during the Communist regime. Even interested people are often of the opinion that Hungarians are Slavs and that Lithuanians and Latvians speak Polish or Russian. These facts are common knowledge to the people of Europe, but how could Americans know these things? Schools do not teach them, and the newspapers are more interested in a recent rape in Florida than in the economic, political, and cultural situations of their neighbors in Mexico or Canada.

American television does not help much. "Headline News" and "CNN" provide information about the rest of the world on a regular basis, but the major networks do not, unless, as we discover in the print media, there is news of a sensational nature. Local television stations inform mostly on local crimes or local economic and political happenings, such as the daily whereabouts of the president or governor. For local television, the world is further restricted, ending at the borders of the county.

Every teacher can provide many examples of the blatantly inadequate knowledge of many Americans about the world beyond the county. I offer two examples. An intelligent female student in a course, Principles of Sociology, was very active during the discussions and once volunteered to present a report based on a selection from Emile Durkheim. She came to me before the presentation and complained that it was too difficult. She had happened on a foreign word, *solidarity.* She was even unable to pronounce the word correctly. She did not understand and was curious to know why Durkheim had used the word, which was coined much later, somewhere in Eastern Europe, to describe a political movement. She could not recall the context in which she first learned of the word and, further, in her own town, there was no such thing as "solidarity."

A second example is about another intelligent female, a minority student enrolled in my course, Race and Ethnic Relations. After two weeks of the semester she came to me with a problem: How is it possible that some other students are able to answer some of my questions about racial and ethnic situations in the United States if these particular issues were not presented in the textbook? She was very sad because she knew everything about her town and actually believed that nothing was different than it was in her own social milieu.

During my current visit to the United States, I have, in addition to teaching at the university, been studying a Polish community in a relatively small town. Both as a university professor and as a researcher, I participated in many parties of a more-or-less formal nature that were organized by individuals and various institutions. Nearly always, I went to these parties with my wife. Two things stand out from these gatherings. One was the way people greeted us. Sometimes we simply said hello, but most of the time we shook hands. But, by "we," I mean only myself and the host. Never that I recall, during the entire year, was my wife offered a hand in greeting or farewell. At the beginning, she was quite offended but then began to accept it as a local custom. I am certain that no one intended to offend her. Everyone was friendly to both of us. Why was she treated differently? Was it sexism? I inquired to learn if someone could explain and was told that this was a kind of custom. We do have different customs in Poland.

Another thing that surprised me was that private parties, but not formal dinner parties, were nearly always of the potluck character. The guests were expected to bring their own beverages and specialties. This does not happen in Poland. One may bring flowers (in the United States, women seemed to be deeply embarrassed when I brought them flowers) and/or a bottle of wine, vodka, or brandy. *No one* brings food. The host would be offended. But in America, not only do people bring food but they can take the leftovers home. Many years ago, the first time I experienced this custom, I did not know what to say. I had brought a bottle of very good Polish vodka to an American friend, but it was too strong for the participants of the party. The people tasted it, perhaps out of courtesy. When I departed, the host gave me the bottle, nearly full, to take with me. For a long time I did not know if I was given a message that I had brought something bad or improper. The next time, I brought a six-pack of beer and we drank all of it.

There was an additional surprise in store for me. My wife and I organized a potluck party for my departmental colleagues. One couple brought a homemade cake. Because they had to leave earlier than the other guests, they asked my wife to give them what remained of their cake. My wife was shocked. The fault was clearly mine. I forgot to tell her what to expect.

When I studied the Polish-American community, I participated in more formal dinners, as well. Some dinners were held by upper-middle-class associations of men and women. Sometimes, but rarely, these dinners were organized in restaurants. Mostly, however, dinners were served in large Polish-American clubs. Participants were dressed up: Men, mostly professionals or from the business community, were in suits; the women wore elegant dresses. The "equipment" was of a different nature. The tables were simple, the table cloths were of paper, and the plates were paper or plastic, as were the glasses. There were no separate plates for dessert. Dessert was thrown on next to the roast beef and potatoes. After dinner, the disposable plates and glasses were rolled into the table cloth and discarded. After dinner, coffee was drunk sitting at a formica table.

This is obviously an example of American efficiency and convenience. Paper table coverings and plastic plates, knives, forks, spoons, and glasses are always in evidence. Now, here in America, we have potluck lunches at work, and now my wife and I also use the products of American chemical expertise when we throw a party. The difference is that, for us, the use of the fake stuff is a problem, especially when the real stuff is so readily available. And, having noticed the dish-washing machines in most of the private houses, we are further confused.

I am led to wonder. American ingenuity, from all quarters addressed to labor-saving devices, serves to free its citizens from the tedious and time-consuming labors of everyday life. This provides free time, perhaps more free time than available in any complex, industrialized society. Why don't Americans devote a portion of this free time to learning something more about the world within and without their own provincial borders?

NOTE

I would like to thank my wife, Maria Nawojczyk, and my brother, Waclaw Mucha, for their helpful comments with this paper.

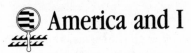 America and I

HERVÉ VARENNE
Teachers College, Columbia University

Having been a foreign graduate student at a prestigious American university, Professor Varenne reflects on differing interpretations of his own personal experiences. What others may have perceived as culture shock was anything but: There were more pressing issues, more important concerns. Now, after twenty years as a resident analyst of American culture, the professional outsider takes a penetrating look into the inside.

Hervé Varenne *was born and raised in France, where he completed his B.A. before earning his doctorate in Anthropology from the University of Chicago in 1972. He is the author of many books and articles on aspects of everyday life and education in the United States. His publications include* Americans Together *(Teachers College Press 1977),* American School Language *(Irvington 1983), and* Ambiguous Harmony *(Ablex, forthcoming). Professor Varenne is the editor and major contributor to* Symbolizing America *(University of Nebraska Press 1986). He is professor of Education at Teachers College, Columbia University.*

Many years after I finished graduate school at the University of Chicago, a friend who had started the same year I did, said something like, "Wow, you were in quite a state of culture shock that year!" My Michigan-born wife still tells me how poignant to her are the stories I tell of my eating my evening meals by myself, alone at a big table for eight at the International House, even when a group of my peers were loudly congregating in another part of the cafeteria. After all, I tell her, they had never specifically invited me, and anyway, I did not really feel comfortable in the midst of a group that seemed so assured of itself, noisily engaging in discussions in which I could not quite take part.

By the time people gave me these interpretations of my behavior, I had thoroughly learned what "culture shock" is meant to refer to in anthropological theory, and I was well versed in all the writings that highlight the difficulties "people from different cultures" have when they meet and have to do something together.

But that is now. Then, the time was September 1968; I was twenty years old. I had spent most of the preceding academic year in Chicago in the shadow of my parents. We had made a comfortable nest that nicely filtered whatever was radically alien. We enjoyed ourselves. As for me, the heavy stakes were back in France where the important exams awaited me. I do not remember having sweated over my application to graduate school in anthropology. No one in my kin or acquaintance had ever applied to any American university. I did not understand the honor that had been given me when I was accepted, and I had no idea of the price I would have to pay.

By October 1968, everything was clearer. I was petrified with the fear that came with the recognition that I was among a very select few and that soon we would be much fewer. I was probably frozen in a quasi-catatonic silence. I now also suspect that it would be easy to analyze conversations with my fellow students and emphasize all the moments when I failed to recognize an invitation to join a group for dinner and all the moments when my requests for an invitation were ignored.

Yet I remember clearly that interactional mismatches were not my most pressing problems. My pressing problem was making sense of Talcott Parsons and of the ways in which my professor David Schneider agreed and disagreed with what he made us read. There I was, with several hundred pages to read a week—something I had never had to do in my college years in France—and three or four important papers to write within the next ten weeks. These assignments were important in all sorts of practical ways: My scholarship was on the line, as was the support my parents were giving me and my evolving recognition that cultural anthropology was something in which I was indeed passionately interested. I may not have fully understood what David Schneider had to say, but my cultural insensitivity to his ways of saying was the least of my concerns.

Eventually, my main concern was alleviated. The year finished and my scholarship was renewed. I was on my way, and I could go for a pure vacation in France as the children of the French petite bourgeoisie always do. The following year I wrote an M.A. thesis, my proposal was accepted, I received a grant, and, after the ritual vacation, I "went into the field" in the bright yellow Pontiac convertible of my childhood dreams about America.

CULTURE SHOCK?

Can one be in "culture shock" and not know it? That depends, of course, on what one means by "culture shock," and thus, eventually, by "culture." Anthropologists generally define *culture shock* as a psychological syndrome, an actual state of a person when he or she is first confronted with the practical recognition that people do not all conduct their everyday life the way he or she has seen people conduct it until then. I still remember the way my heart clutched when I first got a glimpse of American suburbia from the Dan Ryan expressway in Chicago. It corresponded exactly to all the pictures I had seen of it in France, but now these little one-storied houses with their open front yards on tree-lined streets were all around me. They had moved from the world of my imagination to the world of my experience. They were now "here" and not "there."

And so my heart clutched. Often, I was unable and unwilling to perform acts that were routine to most people around me. Like many who first arrive in the United States, I had problems with forms of address. I gagged on calling my professors "Paul," "Cliff," "David," "Milton," and "Vic." My professors could only be "Friedrich," "Geertz," "Schneider," "Singer," and "Turner" in reference (as they still are to me when I talk or think about them) and "Professor . . ." in address (as I have stopped doing in deference to my understanding of American cultural proprieties). Fellow students could be addressed by their first names (but I often referred to them by their last). If I overheard them address professors by their first names, I inferred a familiarity that amounted to a professional anointment: I instinctively assumed that they could do so only because they had already been told that they had passed all the exams that would certify them as "the best." It took me several years to realize that professors could let students address them by their first name, still give them an extremely hard time, and eventually fail them.

These assumptions of mine, and the actual performances that accompanied them, could be interpreted as symptoms of something real that I could not name but that professionals might have helped me through. My friends had seen me, they had talked, and they had made a diagnosis: I was in "culture shock." Like depression or dyslexia, culture shock was an aspect of the world that human beings had failed to locate properly until science "discovered" the syndrome on its way to finding a cure for it.

There is also another possibility that an anthropologist must consider, and that is the possibility that culture shock is something that is "made in America" with miscellaneous pieces of human behavior that would be ignored anywhere else. Certainly I experienced something driving down Dan Ryan expressway that was not fully comfortable, and an empathetic therapist might have made me talk about it. Certainly, it appeared to my friends that I was puzzled, lost, silenced. America offers a pattern to bring all these things together, and they can be made into something that looks like culture shock. But this practical act of my friends when they used this pattern cannot be taken as evidence of a state of *my* mind. At most it is an indicator of what my friends could do—whether they were indeed aware of the logic of their act, whether they in fact believed in culture shocks. Other people in other parts of the world have institutionalized other ways of dealing with the odd behavior of the strangers they receive, and there is little evidence that the American organization of these manifestations more closely approximates "reality" than theirs do.

As far as I was concerned, I did not organize my various experiences in such a way as to recognize "culture shock" as something I was suffering from. I had other problems, and they centered on academic and economic issues. The more I sat in classes and the more I was certain I wanted to continue, the clearer it became that I indeed had a problem here. It was a familiar problem. I had sweated through five sets of major exams in France, and the part of my world in the United States that had to do with academic stuff was not so different. I recognized the fear, and I identified where it came from and what might resolve the problem: persistence. Four years later, I received a Ph.D., I was offered a position as an assistant professor at Teachers College, I married a woman who had been raised fifty miles from the town where I had conducted my fieldwork, and I moved to New York City. I was twenty-four years old then, something I sometimes have to downplay when people around me talk about the great advantage of taking breaks in one's education, experiencing the world, growing, and so on. I had graduated to a new set of problems as I worked toward tenure and at becoming an acceptable husband and father.

Would this four-year journey through the University of Chicago have been easier if I had been born in the middle-class areas of the United States whence came most of my friends? Many anthropologists would initially have to answer "yes" to this question. Individuals have cultures. They feel more comfortable in their own culture. They thrive best there, and they will experience great difficulty when they move to a "new" culture. Such statements have now become common sense, not simply among some anthropologists but also among the people of the United States at large. The anthropologist Michael Moffat once wrote that it may indeed be more enlightened to deal with foreigners through the constructs of culture difference ("After all, he has a different culture, so he can't understand what we are talking about") than through the constructs of intelligence ("He is really dumb").

Still, I believe I had a much easier time at the University of Chicago than many of my friends. Many of them now appear to me much more confused than I was about the fundamental condition of our life there. Then, of course, I thought they were the best and the brightest. After two or three years of studying America, I began to suspect that they could not see through the logic of liberal democracy, or perhaps that they could not organize their own behavior in terms of the vague understanding they must have had that things were not quite working the way they were dramatized to be. When our professors told us that they were treating us "like junior colleagues," they failed to specify that the basic condition of life for a junior assistant professor is (not) getting tenure. Democracy is about races on level fields and about fair competition among formal equals—it is not about universal success. Although every person may become president of the United States, most people will fail. For the vast majority of people in democracies, the fear of failure at the hands of personal interlocutors is the basic condition of everyday life. From the earliest, the persons that may be the closest and most familiar—parents, kindergarten teachers, Little League coaches, peers, and so on—are also the persons who can decide that we are not quite making it, that we need "help," "therapy," a "special" program, an environment "better suited to our needs." At school, on the job, and in most other endeavors, a middle-class person will continually be evaluated and, after a while, evaluating. Democracy is about the daily experience of inequality. In the long run, to mistake an attempt to make the competition fair (by evaluators making themselves "open," "friendly," "personable," and so on) for a sign that one has won is to leave oneself open to major difficulties when the race is actually run and announcements of the prizes are made.

THANKSGIVINGS

I am not so sure that I was in culture shock. From my point of view (and by comparison to my experiences in France), the faculty at Chicago were particularly nice in performing their appointed tasks, and I felt privileged when, in one instance, I could establish another kind of familiarity: the hierarchical familiarity of the adopted son who must continue to demonstrate the confidence his father has placed in him.

In any event, I had a few good friends. I could have extended conversations about structuralism, functionalism, models in the muddles, and other esoterica. I could ask what became and remains the fundamental question of my academic work: How can it make sense for someone to say, or do, this or that? What are the conditions that make this statement or sequence of behavior a reasonable response? What are the costs of other possible responses? How could someone perform something unexpected and not have it noticed as unexpected? In other words, how can one lie? How can one make something that had not been there before? How, perhaps, can one who is not American make it through the University of Chicago?

There happens to be another American myth about the fate of foreigners when they cross the boundaries of the United States. This is the myth of the immigrant who comes with nothing—not even the language—and "makes good" through hard work, self-reliance, and, perhaps, intelligence. This myth is now enshrined in the sacred space of Ellis Island. This is the myth now told about immigrants from the Far East or certain Caribbean islands. This is the myth that explains what is taken to be the success of Asian students in American universities, and it is tempting for me to couch my experience in these terms. I, too, did not speak English well when I came (through the corridors of Kennedy Airport rather than the halls of Ellis Island); I, too, worked hard. And I too made it into the upper ranks of my chosen profession. And so I could celebrate (as in fact I do) the institutions (enlightened admission procedures, generous scholarship funds, understanding professors, and so on) that made it possible for what I must be too modest to call my "talents" to flourish. For this and for many other gifts, I must give thanks every next to last Thursday of November.

There is enough verisimilitude in the Pilgrims' myth to couch my history in the United States in its terms. Still, like all myths, this particular origin myth tells us more about America and what it highlights and downplays than it tells about the experience of immigrants—except as the contents of this myth slowly become an aspect of their conditions that immigrants cannot ignore. For me, as perhaps for many immigrants, including the original Pilgrims, the United States started as the ideal of what France should be but, for whatever reason, could not achieve: a place where an intellectual interest in how human beings live could be comfortably served, with easily accessible libraries, concerned professors, financial help, and so on.

Only later did I understand that all this came at a price. The United States is not simply a more efficient version of France. It is a different place altogether, a different culture, and one cannot accept its gifts without also becoming a part of it. My first Thanksgivings were wonderful anthropological times when I was confronted with stylized, if not ritualized, dramatic performances that revealed America to me in its glory even when the actual details were altogether gross. There was the slightly ridiculous turkey, the continual tellings of overeating, the football games, the plateful of messy mush, and the interactional and physical struggles around the organization and realization of the event (at whose house? on what plane? with whose money?). Thanksgiving is not an easy time for most people in the United States, but it is also a moment of great social unison, a moment reimprovised in individual families, a ritual of beginnings and temporary endings, and a moment when the American spirit is celebrated and reconstituted, even as resources are redistributed.

Thanksgiving is a more encompassing product of America than the other sacred celebration of origins myth, the Fourth of July. I continue to delight in analyzing it, but I also know that it is now "my" myth too—that is, a myth that is being used all around me, for me, and possible against me. For my first two Thanksgivings at the University of Chicago, I was invited by a wonderful association with its headquarters in, of all places for a French man, Paris, Illinois, to come and spend the four days in a home there. Hundreds of certified "foreign students" in Chicago were picked up in buses and driven to various small towns of "downstate Illinois." The families, we were told, would "share their gifts" with us on Thanksgiving day. Only much later did I understand how this event itself recapitulated American culture in a manner that traditional social structural anthropologists would have loved. We stopped at all the sacred spots—including the "Second" Baptist Church, which happened to be our one contact with blacks in Paris. We attended a basketball game at the high school, we visited farms and a small factory, and we were formally asked where we wanted to go to church on Sunday and were taken there. Everything was perfect. There was an inside and there was an outside. My hosts and I safely constructed me as being "outside"—or so I thought.

I am not a certifiable foreigner anymore, and some look at me in a funny way when I tell them that I am not a citizen. After all, I have resided in the United States for more than 20 years; I married an American citizen and have three children who are all citizens; and I am a full professor at a major university. Even if I wished to place myself "out" when the time to give thanks for America comes, I would not get much cooperation. If I ever feel that I have "become" American, I will make the declaration of faith, the pledge of allegiance, the final statement of willingness to be born again civically in a process aptly named "naturalization."

There are many reasons why I will not take this step, why I cannot recite the immigrant myth any more than I can recite the "culture shock" myth. I cannot deny, however, the reality of the myth as something that concerns me. For a long time, I may have deceived myself into thinking that, because I was placed in the position of "foreigner to America," I was free of it. I know better now. From the day when I first entered an American consulate in Marseille and began to respond to the practical requests of the culture, I have been "caught" in America. I yielded, and I continue to yield. I filled out the form and submitted to the medical exams. Later, I became fluent in English to the point that I cannot quite talk anthropology in French. Professionally, I have tried to be an "accessible" faculty member who addresses his students by their first names and lets them address him by his first name. I laugh understandingly when people talk about the state of culture shock I was in or about the way I still have a French accent, a French writing style, and a French way of arguing. I was never coerced. Indeed, I can say that I have chosen to remain caught by America. To tell the truth, when I was finally fully surrounded by America during my fieldwork in Appleton, I discovered that I fundamentally liked this culture and that I enjoyed the cultural manifestations that many of my student friends, at the end of the 1960s, were struggling so hard to escape.

AMERICA AS FACT

Enjoying America does not make an American. It does not make me one, and it does not make anyone else one either. This is the anthropologist, the professional outsider, speaking. Neither I nor anybody else in the United States can be explained by culture shock and its attendant psychointeractional traumas. I cannot be explained through the myth of the immigrant.

Still, both myths are real conditions of my life here. "American culture" is as present to me, and to everyone else in the United States, as the Atlantic Ocean, and I know by experience that landing at Kennedy airport is not much different from plunging into water: Certain specific things had better be done fast if one does not want to drown (or be shipped back to the old country). It is not the case that America is real because all of us in the United States "believe" it is real. America and its myths, rituals, customs, and institutions are real because people persist in placing us in conditions where we have to respond practically to the conditions according to their own logic.

Take a question like "Why are you not getting naturalized?" or a statement like "I guess you do not understand what we are trying to say because you are not from this country." The people who tell me such things are themselves caught in a cultural web that makes these statements commonsensical to the people who utter them. These questions and statements then become an aspect of the cultural web in which I now have to perform. I can make many different responses; I can even ignore the question. But other people will respond to me in the terms set by the question, and it will indeed make more sense to try and construct an answer—particularly if I expect to stay in the good graces of the people who asked the question. To the question about naturalization, I usually answer that I will not change citizenship because I believe that nationalism is one of the most dangerous ideas evolved by the human species (more dangerous than the atomic bomb). I believe that the process of changing citizenship puts a focus on nationalism and thus reinforces the institutions of nationalism that I wish to undermine. I cannot help being a French citizen because the current international order is based on every human being on the globe "having" a nationality. But I can choose not to carry an American passport.

This is a plausible answer even though many in the United States who have given a different answer, or who are the descendants of people who gave a different answer, do not like it. After all, the most powerful political statement of the 1960s was not "Make love, not war." It was "America, love it or leave it." Note, that to be meaningful, both statements depend on joining the concept of love with a proper social unit—couple, family, state, and country—for which one must eventually give thanks. This is the frame within which questions about one's relationship to America are placed, and to the extent that one cannot prevent the questions from being asked, this is the frame within which one's own answers, behaviors, and life history are placed; cross-referenced with other answers, behaviors, and life histories; and then evaluated.

I have been writing that I was "placed in the position of an outsider" rather than "I was an outsider," for precisely the reason that the framing of my actions, during my first years in the United States as well as now, has never been under my control. I was free not to apply for a visa to come to the country, but once I decided to apply, I placed myself within one of the categories defined by Congress and the State Department. So I got a "student visa," which gave me special rights, privileges, duties, and limitations. When I went to Paris, Illinois, on my Thanksgiving trips, the fact that I had such a category was used, by both myself and my hosts, as the essential aspect of my history that justified my trip. Once in Paris, the formal differences between my hosts and myself were further expanded: In their speech, their behavior, and their actions, they and I improvised a particular version of "the foreign student." That this was a special time tightly controlled by American patterns is perhaps best revealed by the experience of students from sub-Saharan Africa. In the practices of the town, they were, precisely, *not* black, and they were given access to parts of homes that other people of African descent never touched—except perhaps as domestics.

Later, when I finally received my doctorate, I could have left the United States. To stay, I had to redefine myself, administratively at first. And so I was a "resident alien." With this status, I was moved out of the position of outsider. My story was recast as it could now be said that I was "one of those foreign students who say they want to return home at the end of their studies but always find a way of staying here." There are flattering versions of this story and not so flattering ones. I never can quite control which version is going to be told when, and I may try desperately to argue—as I am doing here—that there is more to me than such stories. But I cannot prevent such stories from being told in the particular ways that make America unique and altogether beautiful.

FUTURES: PATHS NOT YET TAKEN

Cultural anthropology, uncomfortably, has a place within the behavioral *sciences*. What it writes about the fate of human beings when they get together is eventually judged by its power to enlighten us about the universal processes that are involved in the production of uniquely particular moments. What I write about America, to the extent that I consider myself a scientist of sorts, I could write about France. France, too, is a historically developed frame, a set of patterns used in France to handle the social world the French—and all others who cross the boundaries of the country—get to inhabit. The history of France has been different from the history of the United States, and the cultural worlds that have evolved in each geographical and institutional space are different. Not only are they different, but they are also at work maintaining a difference, since—as time has passed—each has become part of the historical reality of the other. America, for a long time, was a reproach to France ("Why can't we be like them?"). France, or at least the vague vision of Europe that may cross the Atlantic, can be, for America, either a cautionary tale about what people escaped, a reference point to measure "how far we have gone," or—more recently—an occasion to worry about competitors.

What one says, writes, and does is always framed by a cultural pattern that offers the phonology, vocabulary, syntax, rhetoric, style, and genre in which the statement could be expressed. As the Russian philosopher of language, Mikhail Bakhtin, wrote, we always speak in borrowed words on a marketplace crowded with others also struggling to make themselves heard over our own voices. I take this to be a major finding of scientific research in anthropology and sociology. No statement, however framed, is ever *determined* by its frame. Indeed, all statements are, wittingly or not, challenges to the frame, attempts to say more than is allowed by a stereotypical application of the pattern.

Certainly, here, I am writing in English, in the style of a quasi-scholarly paper, within the framework of anthropology, and so on. It would, however, be more accurate to my condition to say that I am struggling with all that has been given me to say something that will move us along. Whether it does is not really in my hands. As such a paper is read, it becomes a more or less temporary or powerful moment in the history of the reader. It may be disregarded or may cause one to stumble as one moves along one's path. It may also move someone to notice another path or to open another one. This response itself may then become a possibility for me. It may be ignored, or it may lead to a further reframing of my own life.

Nothing is standing still in human life. Neither America nor I, each as historical facts—albeit of an incommensurably different scale—can control each other or even our own future. We can answer questions about what was done, about the process through which things get done, but not about what is going to get done. There is no definite answer to that question except the one found in a famous phrase that summarizes best my first experiences of America, a phrase that nicely ties liberal democratic strivings with their biblical roots in their many manifestations: The answer is blowing in the wind.

A Cross-Cultural Experience: A Chinese Anthropologist in the United States

HUANG SHU-MIN
Iowa State University

Using a variety of interesting and sometimes humorous encounters with Americans, Professor Huang Shu-min describes how these experiences can lead to a better understanding of one's own culture. He emphasizes that although these experiences can lead to greater awareness, it is difficult even for anthropologists to free themselves of the assumptions about their own culture.

Huang Shu-min *is a professor of Anthropology at Iowa State University, where he has been teaching since 1975. Born and raised in China and Taiwan, Huang spent much of his research periods in these two regions. He received his B.A. in Anthropology from National Taiwan University (1967) and his M.A. and Ph.D. in Anthropology from Michigan State University (1973, 1977).*

Born and raised in many areas of China, including the Mainland, Hong Kong, and Taiwan, I have developed a deep appreciation for the enormous cultural variations in China. Ever since I can remember, I seemed to have been surrounded by people—including my own family members—who speak many languages and entertain various tastes in food and clothing that characterize regional differences in China.

However, despite my exposure to such a diverse way of life, I was probably brought up as a normal, average Chinese, taught to believe in the traditional Chinese values, manners, and beliefs characteristic of Confucian literati. A reverence for age and custom, a high motivation toward scholarly achievement, and a strong sense of responsibility toward society had all been incorporated into my thinking throughout the process of growth.

Contact with anthropology in my college years in Taiwan, however, brought about basic changes in my life. Anthropology claims that much of our behavior, customs, and even ways of thinking are molded by our culture, which is essentially a set of artificially designed symbols accumulated throughout human history. Accepting such a premise, I began to question the validity and rationale of all the values, beliefs, and even ways of thinking that I once had stood for and cherished. As a consequence, I was, to borrow a phrase from Muriel Dimen-Schein (1977), "drawn to its (anthropology's) moral emphasis that our culture was not the best or only way to live, and alternatives existed." My soul-searching along this line has not led to a total rejection of my culture; rather, I began to develop a habit of looking at my own behavior from an objective point of view and to be critical of things that I had taken for granted.

My career in anthropology has eventually brought me to study and to teach in the United States. Situated in an entirely different culture, I have been able not only to look at my own culture from this objective point of view but also to make a constant comparison between my own cultural practices and those of Americans. To bring my professional training into everyday situations, which involves explaining ordinary events against both the Chinese and American frames of thought, I have tried to explore the extent to which human beings are influenced by their specific cultures. The following incidents have occurred during my residence in the United States and form the foundation for some of my reflections.

INTRODUCTION TO AMERICA

My initiation into American culture was through my older sister, who had lived in San Francisco for some time before I arrived in 1970. Apparently aghast at my appearance when we met at the airport, especially my dandruff-ridden hair and unshaved face, she warned me that Americans are extremely sensitive about physical appearances. I should from then on use dandruff-proof shampoo and shave my face every day—even though there is not much to work on.

I was puzzled by her notions, for I had heard about the counterculture movement in the United States, especially on campuses across the country. My limited knowledge about the counterculture seemed to indicate the development of an alternative way of life, which also implied, to some extent, the rejection of American middle-class values. If that was the case, why bother with this physical appearance–laden life-style? I kept this question to myself, for I thought my sister was just old-fashioned and conservative, and so there was no point in arguing with her.

I stayed in San Francisco for a month, and during that period I made many sightseeing tours around the city. My specific interest was in the hippie ghettoes. As a novice in anthropology, I believed that the counter-culture movement presented a unique opportunity to study how culture can be changed in a well-intentioned manner. Based on my superficial observations, these people appeared to be sincere about developing an alternative way of life in direct opposition to that of middle-class values: long and uncombed hair, bare feet, patched blue jeans and free-floating along the sidewalks, for example.

I was very much impressed by what I saw. But then I suddenly noticed that I had not seen anyone with dandruff. I brought up this question to an acquaintance who was very much involved in this particular way of life. "Oh, yes," he replied in a typically nonchalant manner, "dandruff is indeed a problem to many of us. But we use dandruff-proof shampoo."

Disappointed? No. It only confirmed an idea that I had but could not prove with evidence: While we may claim to reject our culture's values and moral standards en masse, in the deeper layer of the heart and mind, our thinking and behavior may still operate, even though unconsciously, under the same set of beliefs.

CULTURE AND HAIR COLOR

My graduate years at Michigan State University were some of the most interesting experiences during my time at school. We had a large student body—thirty-odd in my first-year class. A great number of my classmates were from different nations, and many of the other American students also had had personal experiences in other parts of the world. We formed a very close group, often having parties, picnics, and other activities together.

One day after class, we stayed in the classroom chatting about recent events. Suddenly, someone in the group mentioned the long absence of a female classmate: "Strange, I have not seen the little redhead for the past few days!"

Little redhead? The notion did not ring a bell at all. How could he refer to someone in such a strange way? Did this person really have red hair? Why had I never noticed this? I took a hard look around the classroom and realized that there were indeed different hair styles and colors among my classmates, something that I had never paid attention to!

The discovery that Americans frequently divide their hair into categories and use this taxonomical difference as a point of reference was something entirely new to me. Chinese would never refer to another person by describing his or her hair, for every Chinese has dark, straight hair, except the aged and bald. Because hair is an insignificant difference, Chinese probably do not have an acute conceptual system to categorize people on the basis of hair traits and, as a consequence, tend to neglect this physical characteristic entirely.

PRIMARY AND SECONDARY LANGUAGES

One incident that happened before I came to the States puzzled me for some time. In 1969, I was working with Professor and Mrs. Gallin in Taipei, studying rural migrants in the city. One day my father came to see me and also had a chat with Professor Gallin. Because my father does not speak English and his Mandarin has an accent that Professor Gallin could not quite follow, I had to serve as translator in the conversation. When my father spoke to me for the translation, I noticed that he used Taiwanese (or Min-nan), the native language in Taiwan, instead of the Mandarin or Cantonese that we normally use. Even though my father and I speak flawless Taiwanese, we never use it in our direct, personal conversation.

So, I mildly reminded my father that because Professor Gallin is not a Taiwanese, and because he was talking to him through me, there was no need to use this particular language. My suggestion was to no avail, and my father kept speaking to me in Taiwanese. After a few more protests, I decided to ignore it, thinking that my father was probably too excited by speaking to a "foreign barbarian."

When studying in Michigan, a similar incident occurred, which rekindled my old puzzlement. One day I was in the Gallins' house when another professor came for a visit and brought with him an Austrian friend. It was late in the afternoon, and we all decided to stay for dinner at the Gallins' invitation. Over the dinner table, Professor Gallin talked to this Austrian visitor about some general things, and suddenly he spoke in Chinese to this Austrian. He said, *"Ch'ing-lai, puke-ch'i,"* which literally means, "Please help yourself; don't be polite." Unaware of this slip of the tongue, Professor Gallin continued the conversation in English.

These two incidents led me to theorize that cognition probably operates on several planes. The first and probably the most "instinctive" cognitive plane involves a person's primary language and the intimate way of life and cultural values in which one is brought up. Beyond this are the secondary and tertiary planes, which involve bodies of knowledge of foreign cultures. So when people encounter another person who does not belong to their primary cognitive community, they would probably immediately project their secondary or tertiary cognitive systems to this person, thinking that would fit the circumstance. If my hypothesis is correct, then there would be nothing unusual if we see a student majoring in Spanish who tries to communicate with a Japanese tourist in Spanish!

WHAT NOT TO SAY

It is a custom for Chinese to say something auspicious when two newly met friends part. Phrases like "Wish you make a fortune," or "Wish you success in your business" (or study, voyage, and so on) are appropriate on such occasions. Because in traditional China marriage was often arranged by parents, it was quite common for one to greet a couple in love with a phrase like "Wish you marry soon"—meaning that this couple would convince their parents to accept their own choice. This kind of greeting is still commonly used in Taiwan, and I suspect it is also true in Hong Kong, although to a lesser extent. But, used in a different cultural context, this kind of expression may cause some problems.

Once I was invited to a party in which the American host and hostess entertained a couple of their friends and some Chinese students. We were introduced to the host's younger sister and her boyfriend—both were college students and had lived together for some time. They professed their emotional attachment toward each other and also indicated their suspicion concerning the meaning of a formal marriage: "We prefer our current arrangement," said the young man. "If two persons really love each other, there is no need to bind them together with some kind of socially sanctioned contract."

It was a pleasant evening, and about the time we were to leave, a Chinese student approached the young lovers and inadvertently said, "Wish to see you marry soon!"

He probably did not literally mean what he had said nor even realize what he had said. But the reaction from this young couple was obvious. The young man was stunned and stood there with a stiffened mouth. Blushing, the young woman protested, "But we don't believe in marriage!"

FOOD

One aspect of American culture that I have not been able to develop full appreciation of is food. Brought up in a culture whose menu contains a wide range of food varieties and flavors, I consider American food rather plain. And, worst of all, when I have American meals, I often feel full rather quickly, sometimes after just the salad. But then in a short while, I will feel hungry.

Originally, I thought that this was a phenomenon peculiar to me, mainly because I do not have a taste for American food and hence cannot eat too much of it. Believing that Chinese dishes have a better taste than anything else, I never had the slightest idea that Americans could have the same problem when eating Chinese food.

One day, my wife and I invited a few colleagues of mine over for supper. Our conversation somehow had focused on food preparation in different cultures. I jokingly remarked that even though I am an anthropologist by training, my appetite does not really match my intellectual capacity. I told them of the peculiar problem I had in eating American meals and indicated the possible reason as I saw it. On hearing that, one of our guests burst into laughter. "This is exactly the same problem I have when I come to your house for dinner," he said. "Even though I am quite full now, I will be very hungry by the time I arrive home. And I used to think this was so because of the strange taste of Chinese food!" I was surprised to find that the same opinion was shared by others.

I was puzzled by this cross-cultural eating problem. Perhaps the differences in taste are not the cause of the problem. Comparing dietary differences between American and Chinese food from another angle, I began to realize that food variety and content is the main difference between them. Chinese food contains many starchy items, such as rice, bean products, and vegetables, while American food has more meat tissue. When eating meals, the human digestive system probably has certain expectations on the quantity of specific items habitually established in the culture. People may feel full when the quota for certain food items has been met but still feel hungry for the unmet ones. For that reason, we may all have problems eating a cross-cultural meal.

A COMPLEX PHENOMENON

Human culture is a complex phenomenon: It provides a way of life, cues for actions, and logic for reasoning for the members of a cultural community. Because we frequently all too strongly adhere to our own culture, we fail to understand or appreciate the alternative ways of life. It is not an easy task to eliminate the cultural bias that hinders a mutual understanding across cultural boundaries. Even among anthropologists, who claim to study human cultures objectively, the same kind of prejudices persist, for we are products of our unique cultures as are any other human beings. Anthropologists may be credited for providing a large amount of literature describing the "other cultures." But perhaps more is needed. Other cultures may serve as a mirror for us to look at our own practices as culture-bound human beings. We need to be as critical of our own ways of thinking, value standards, and behavior patterns as we are of the cultures that we study. It is hoped that, by such a consistent practice of self-examination, we may come to understand the deeper meaning of culture on a first-hand basis.

ACKNOWLEDGMENT

I am grateful to Professor and Mrs. Bernard Gallin, both at Michigan State University, for introducing me to anthropology and American culture. Appreciations are also due to my colleagues and associates at Iowa State

University, especially those who were involved in the course, "Cross-Cultural Exploration: Introduction to the Third World." Most of my ideas and reflections were discussed and developed in that class.

REFERENCE

DIMEN-SCHEIN, MURIEL
1977   The Anthropological Imagination. New York: McGraw-Hill.

SIX

The Young, the Rich, and the Famous: Individualism as an American Cultural Value

P O R A N E E   N A T A D E C H A - S P O N S E L
University of Hawaii, Honolulu

From the point of view of a scholar raised in Thailand, Americans appear open and immediately friendly in their greetings. However, if one looks closely with a critical eye, these greetings are superficial and ritualized, and they tend to hide the more important aspects of American cultural values. The openness in greetings provides both contrast and contradiction to the closedness of social relations and family structures, especially when compared to traditional Thai cultural values. Further, the values of privacy and individualism and the attainment of wealth and fame are viewed as critical elements in relation to the nature of social relations and the kinship system.

Poranee Natadecha-Sponsel *was born and raised in the multiethnic region of Thais and Malays in the southern part of Thailand. Poranee has lived in the United States for over fifteen years. She received her B.A. with Honors in English and Philosophy from Chulalongkorn University in Bangkok, Thailand (1969). She earned her M.A. in Philosophy at Ohio University, Athens (1973), and her Ed.D. (1991), from the University of Hawaii at Mānoa, is in Educational Foundations with an interdisciplinary focus on Anthropology and Environmental Education. She currently teaches interdisciplinary courses in Women's Studies and coordinates the Mentoring Program for New Women Faculty at the University of Hawaii at Mānoa.*

Hi, how are you?" "Fine, thank you, and you?" These are greetings that everybody in America hears and says every day—salutations that come ready-made and packaged just like a hamburger and fries. There is no real expectation for any special information in response to these greetings. Do not, under any circumstances, take up anyone's time by responding in depth to the programmed query. What or how you may feel at the moment is of little, if any, importance. Thai people would immediately perceive that our concerned American friends are truly interested in our welfare, and this concern would require polite reciprocation by spelling out the details of our current condition. We become very disappointed when we have had enough experience in the United States to learn that we have bored, amused, or even frightened many of our American acquaintances by taking the greeting "How are you?" so literally. We were reacting like Thai, but in the American context where salutations have a different meaning, our detailed reactions were inappropriate. In Thai society, a greeting among acquaintances usually requests specific information about the other person's condition, such as "Where are you going?" or "Have you eaten?"

One of the American contexts in which this greeting is most confusing and ambiguous is at the hospital or clinic. In these sterile and ritualistic settings, I have always been uncertain exactly how to answer when the doctor or nurse asks "How are you?" If I deliver a packaged answer of "Fine," I wonder if I am telling a lie. After all, I am there in the first place precisely because I am not so fine. Finally, after debating for some time, I asked one nurse how she expected a patient to answer the query "How are you?" But after asking this question, I then wondered if it was rude to do so. However, she looked relieved after I explained to her that people from different cultures have different ways to greet other people and that for me to be asked how I am in the hospital results in awkwardness. Do I simply answer, "Fine, thank you," or do I reveal in accurate detail how I really feel at the moment? My suspicion was verified when the nurse declared that "How are you?" was really no more than a polite greeting and that she didn't expect any answer more elaborate than simply "Fine." However, she told me that some patients do answer her by describing every last ache and pain from which they are suffering.

A significant question that comes to mind is whether the verbal pattern of greetings reflects any social relationship in American culture. The apparently warm and sincere greeting may initially suggest interest in the person, yet the intention and expectations are, to me, quite superficial. For example, most often the person greets you quickly and then walks by to attend to other business without even waiting for your response! This type of greeting is just like a package of American fast food! The person eats the food quickly without enjoying the taste. The convenience is like many other American accoutrements of living such as cars, household appliances, efficient telephones, or simple, systematic, and predictable arrangements of groceries in the supermarket. However, usually when this greeting is delivered, it seems to lack a personal touch and genuine feeling. It is little more than ritualized behavior.

I have noticed that most Americans keep to themselves even at social gatherings. Conversation may revolve around many topics, but little, if anything, is revealed about oneself. Without talking much about oneself and not knowing much about others, social relations seem to remain at an abbreviated superficial level. How could one know a person without knowing something about him or her? How much does one need to know about a person to really know that person?

After living in this culture for more than a decade, I have learned that there are many topics that should not be mentioned in conversations with American acquaintances or even close friends. One's personal life and one's income are considered to be very private and even taboo topics. Unlike my Thai culture, Americans do not show interest or curiosity by asking such personal questions, especially when one just meets the individual for the first time. Many times I have been embarrassed by my Thai acquaintances who recently arrived at the University of Hawaii and the East–West Center. For instance, one day I was walking on campus with an American friend when we met another Thai woman to whom I had been introduced a few days earlier. The Thai woman came to write her doctoral dissertation at the East–West Center where the American woman worked, so I introduced them to each other. The American woman greeted my Thai companion in Thai language, which so impressed her that she felt immediately at ease. At once, she asked the American woman numerous personal questions such as, How long did you live in Thailand? Why were you there? How long were you married to the Thai man? Why did you divorce him? How long have you been divorced? Are you going to marry a Thai again or an American? How long have you been working here? How much do you earn? The American was stunned. However, she was very patient and more or less answered all those questions as succinctly as she could. I was so uncomfortable that I had to interrupt whenever I could to get her out of the awkward situation in which she had been forced into talking about things she considered personal. For people in Thai society, such questions would be appropriate and not considered too personal let alone taboo.

The way Americans value their individual privacy continues to impress me. Americans seem to be open and yet there is a contradiction because they are also aloof and secretive. This is reflected in many of their behavior patterns. By Thai standards, the relationship between friends in American society seems to be somewhat superficial. Many Thai students, as well as other Asians, have felt that they could not find genuine friendship with Americans. For example, I met many American classmates who were very helpful and friendly while we were in the same class. We went out, exchanged phone calls, and did the same things as would good friends in Thailand. But those activities stopped suddenly when the semester ended.

Privacy as a component of the American cultural value of individualism is nurtured in the home as children grow up. From birth they are given their own individual, private space, a bedroom separate from that of their parents. American children are taught to become progressively independent, both emotionally and economically, from their family. They learn to help themselves at an early age. In comparison, in Thailand, when parents bring a new baby home from the hospital, it shares the parents' bedroom for two to three years and then shares another bedroom with older siblings of the same sex. Most Thai children do not have their own private room until they finish high school, and some do not have their own room until another sibling moves out, usually when the sibling gets married. In Thailand, there are strong bonds within the extended family. Older siblings regularly help their parents to care for younger ones. In this and other ways, the Thai family emphasizes the interdependence of its members.

I was accustomed to helping Thai babies who fell down to stand up again. Thus, in America when I saw babies fall, it was natural for me to try to help them back on their feet. Once at a summer camp for East–West Center participants, one of the supervisors brought his wife and their ten-month-old son with him. The baby was so cute that many students were playing with him. At one point he was trying to walk and fell, so all the Asian students, males and females, rushed to help him up. Although the father and mother were nearby, they paid no attention to their fallen and crying baby. However, as the students were trying to help and comfort him, the parents told them to leave him alone; he would be all right on his own. The baby did get up and stopped crying without any assistance. Independence is yet another component of the American value of individualism.

Individualism is even reflected in the way Americans prepare, serve, and consume food. In a typical American meal, each person has a separate plate and is not supposed to share or taste food from other people's plates. My Thai friends and I are used to eating Thai style, in which you share food from a big serving dish in the middle of the table. Each person dishes a small amount from the serving dish onto his or her plate and finishes this portion before going on with the next portion of the same or a different serving dish. With the Thai pattern of eating, you regularly reach out to the serving dishes throughout the meal. But this way of eating is not considered appropriate in comparison to the common American practice where each person eats separately from his or her individual plate.

One time my American host, a divorcée who lived alone, invited a Thai girlfriend and myself to an American dinner at her home. When we were reaching out and eating a small portion of one thing at a time in Thai style, we were told to dish everything we wanted onto our plates at one time and that it was not considered polite to reach across the table. The proper American way was to have each kind of food piled up on your plate at once. If we were to eat in the same manner in Thailand, eyebrows would have been raised at the way we piled up food on our plates, and we would have been considered to be eating like pigs, greedy and inconsiderate of others who shared the meal at the table.

Individualism as a pivotal value in American culture is reflected in many other ways. Material wealth is not only a prime status marker in American society but also a guarantee and celebration of individualism—wealth allows the freedom to do almost anything, although usually within the limits of law. The pursuit of material wealth through individual achievement is instilled in Americans from the youngest age. For example, I was surprised to see an affluent American couple, who own a large ranch house and two BMW cars, send their nine-year-old son to deliver newspapers. He has to get up very early each morning to deliver the papers, even on Sunday! During summer vacation, the boy earns additional money by helping in his parents' gift shop from 10 A.M. to 5 P.M. His thirteen-year-old sister often earns money by babysitting, even at night.

In Thailand, only children from poorer families work to earn money to help the household. Middle- and high-income parents do not encourage their children to work until after they have finished their education. They provide economic support in order to free their children to concentrate on and excel in their studies. Beyond the regular schooling, families who can afford it pay for special tutoring as well as training in music, dance, or sports. However, children in low- and middle-income families help their parents with household chores and the care of younger children.

Many American children have been encouraged to get paid for their help around the house. They rarely get any gifts free of obligations. They even have to be good to get Santa's gifts at Christmas! As they grow up, they are conditioned to earn things they want; they learn that "there is no such thing as a free lunch." From an early age, children are taught to become progressively independent economically from their parents. Also, most young people are encouraged to leave home at college age to be on their own. From my viewpoint as a Thai, it seems that American family ties and closeness are not as strong as in Asian families whose children depend on family financial support until joining the work force after college age. Thereafter, it is the children's turn to help support their parents financially.

Modern American society and economy emphasize individualism in other ways. The nuclear family is more common than the extended family, and newlyweds usually establish their own independent household rather than initially living with either the husband's or the wife's parents. Parents and children appear to be close only when the children are very young. Most American parents seem to "lose" their children by the teenage years. They don't seem to belong to each other as closely as do Thai families. Even though I have seen more explicit affectionate expression among American family members than among Asian ones, the close interpersonal spirit seems to be lacking. Grandparents have relatively little to do with the grandchildren on any regular basis, in contrast to the extended family, which is more common in Thailand. The family and society seem to be graded by age to the point that grandparents, parents, and children are separated by generational subcultures that are evidently alienated from one another. Each group "does its own thing." Help and support are usually limited to whatever does not interfere with one's own life. In America, the locus of responsibility is more on the individual than on the family.

In one case I know of, a financially affluent grandmother with Alzheimer's disease is taken care of twenty-four hours a day by hired help in her own home. Her daughter visits and relieves the helper occasionally. The mature granddaughter, who has her own family, rarely visits. Yet they all live in the same neighborhood. However, each lives in a different house, and each is very independent. Although the mother worries about the grandmother, she cannot do much. Her husband also needs her, and she divides her time between him, her daughters and their children, and the grandmother. When the mother needs to go on a trip with her husband, a second hired attendant is required to care for the grandmother temporarily. When I asked why the granddaughter doesn't temporarily care for the grandmother, the reply was that she has her own life, and it would not be fair for the granddaughter to take care of the grandmother, even for a short period of time. Yet I wonder if it is fair for the grandmother to be left out. It seems to me that the value of individualism and its associated independence account for these apparent gaps in family ties and support.

In contrast to American society, in Thailand older parents with a long-term illness are asked to move in with their children and grandchildren if they are not already living with them. The children and grandchildren take turns attending to the grandparent, sometimes with help from live-in maids. Living together in the same house reinforces moral support among the generations within an extended family. The older generation is respected because of the previous economic, social, and moral support for their children and grandchildren. Family relations provide one of the most important contexts for being a "morally good person," which is traditionally the principal concern in the Buddhist society of Thailand.

In America, being young, rich, and/or famous allows one greater freedom and independence and thus promotes the American value of individualism. This is reflected in the mass appeal of major annual television events like the Super Bowl and the Academy Awards. The goal of superachievement is also seen in more mundane ways. For example, many parents encourage their children to take special courses and to work hard to excel in sports as a shortcut to becoming rich and famous. I know one mother who has taken her two sons to tennis classes and tournaments since the boys were six years old, hoping that at least one of them will be a future tennis star like Ivan Lendl. Other parents focus their children on acting, dancing, or musical talent. The children have to devote much time and hard work as well as sacrifice the ordinary activities of youth in order to develop and perform their natural talents and skills in prestigious programs. But those who excel in the sports and entertainment industries can become rich and famous, even at an early age, as for example Madonna, Tom Cruise, and Michael Jackson. Television and other media publicize these celebrities and thereby reinforce the American value of individualism, including personal achievement and financial success.

Although the American cultural values of individualism and the aspiration to become rich and famous have had some influence in Thailand, there is also cultural and religious resistance to these values. Strong social bonds, particularly within the extended family, and the hierarchical structure of the kingdom run counter to individualism. Also, youth gain social recognition through their academic achievement. From the perspective of Theravada Buddhism, which strongly influences Thai culture, aspiring to be rich and famous would be an illustration of greed, and those who have achieved wealth and fame do not celebrate it publicly as much as in American society. Being a good, moral person is paramount, and ideally Buddhists emphasize restraint and moderation.

Beyond talent and skill in the sports and entertainment industries, there are many other ways that young Americans can pursue wealth. Investment is one route. One American friend who is only a sophomore in college has already invested heavily in the stock market to start accumulating wealth. She is just one example of the 1980s trend for youth to be more concerned with their individual finances than with social, political, and environmental issues. With less attention paid to public issues, the expression of individualism seems to be magnified through emphasis on lucrative careers, financial investment, and material consumption—the "Yuppie" phenomenon. This includes new trends in dress, eating, housing (condominiums), and cars (expensive European imports). Likewise, there appears to be less of a long-term commitment to marriage. More young couples are living together without either marriage or plans for future marriage. When such couples decide to get married, prenuptial agreements are made to protect their assets. Traditional values of marriage, family, and sharing appear to be on the decline.

Individualism as one of the dominant values in American culture is expressed in many ways. This value probably stems from the history of the society as a frontier colony of immigrants in search of a better life with independence, freedom, and the opportunity for advancement through personal achievement. However, in the beliefs and customs of any culture there are some disadvantages as well as advantages. Although Thais may admire the achievements and material wealth of American society, there are costs, especially in the value of individualism and associated social phenomena.

SEVEN

Growing Up American: Doing the Right Thing

AMPARO B. OJEDA
Loyola University, Chicago

As a young student on her first visit to America, Professor Ojeda, a Fulbright scholar, was reassured that her adjustment to American life and culture would be easy. The orientation survival kit was of minimal help in adjusting to some American customs, especially those involving child-rearing. Years later, in returning to the United States with a daughter, Professor Ojeda was faced with a crucial conflict of values—American values versus the more respectful values of her own Philippine traditions.

Amparo B. Ojeda *was born and raised in the Philippines. She completed her undergraduate degree and an M.A. in English Literature from the University of San Carlos, Philippines, and an M.S. in Linguistics from Georgetown University under the Fulbright program. Rudolf R. Rahmann, a Divine Word Missionary (SVD) and an anthropologist, encouraged her to pursue anthropology with a special emphasis in Southeast Asian anthropology and linguistics. She earned her doctorate at the University of San Carlos. Professor Ojeda has conducted fieldwork in the Philippines and is involved in ongoing research on the adjustment of Filipino immigrants in Metropolitan Chicago. She is an associate professor of Anthropology and Linguistics at Loyola University, Chicago.*

The earliest and closest encounter that I had with Americans, and a most superficial brush with their culture, goes back to my childhood days when an American family moved into our neighborhood. I used to gaze at the children, a boy and a girl, who were always neatly dressed and who would romp around their fenced front yard. Not knowing their names, I, together with a cousin, used to call them, *"Hoy, Americano!"* (Hey, American!), and they themselves soon learned to greet us with

"Hey Filipino!" That was as far as our "acquaintance" went because in no time at all they were gone, and we never again heard about them.

That brief encounter aroused my curiosity. I wanted to know something more about the "Americanos." What kind of people are they? What food do they eat? Where is America? As time passed, I learned about America—about the people and about some aspects of their life-style—but my knowledge was indirect. The opportunity to experience the world of the "Americano" directly was long in coming, and when it did I was gripped with a sense of ambivalence. How would I fare in a strange and foreign land with an unfamiliar culture? That was how I finally found myself on the plane that would bring me on the first leg of my cultural sojourn to Hawaii.

Excited as I was, I could hear my heart thumping, and apprehension came over me. Suddenly, the thought hit me: I have journeyed far from home, away from the comforts and familiarity of my culture. You see, in this trip, my first outside of my homeland, I did not come as an anthropologist to do fieldwork. I came as a graduate student to study linguistics. Seven years later I would be an anthropologist. But I am getting ahead of myself.

My host family during my brief two-week stay in Honolulu was waiting at the airport. The whole family was there! The children's beaming faces and the family's warm and gracious greetings gave me a sense of assurance that everything was going to be fine. "There's nothing to it," we Fulbright scholars were reassured during a briefing on aspects of adjustment to American life and culture. So there I was in Hawaii, the first leg of my cultural sojourn (I stayed in the Midwest for another four weeks of orientation, before proceeding east to do graduate work), equipped with a theoretical survival kit designed and guaranteed to work. I would later discover that there were discrepancies between the ideal procedures and techniques and day-to-day behavior.

The differences between my culture and American culture became evident in the first few hours after my arrival. On our way out of the air terminal, the children began to fuss: "I'm hungry," "I'm tired," "I'm thirsty," "I want to go to the bathroom!" Over the whining and fidgeting of the children, my hosts and I tried to carry on a conversation but to no avail. Amazingly, despite the constant interruptions, the adults displayed considerable tolerance and patience. No voice was raised, nor harsh words spoken. I vividly recall how, as children, we were reminded never to interrupt while adults were talking, and to avoid annoying behavior, especially when in the company of adults, whether these people were kin, friends, or strangers.

We left the main highway, drove on a country road, and eventually parked by a Howard Johnson restaurant. The children did not need any bidding at all. They ran inside the restaurant in search of a table for us. I was fascinated by their quite independent and assertive behavior (more of this, later). I had originally been feeling dizzy and drowsy from the long plane ride, but I wasn't anymore. My "cultural" curiosity was aroused by the children's youthful showmanship, or so I thought. As soon as we were all seated, a young man came to hand us menus. The children made their own choices. Not feeling hungry at all, but wanting to show appreciation, I settled for a cup of soup. When the food finally came, I was completely shocked by the portions each child had. I wondered if they could eat it all. Just as I feared, they left their portions only partially eaten. What a waste, I thought. I remembered one of my father's gems of thought: "Take only what you can eat, and make sure to eat the last morsel on your plate." I must confess that I felt very bad looking at mounds of uneaten food. How can so much food be wasted? Why were children allowed to order their food themselves instead of Mom and Dad doing it for them? Was it a part of independence training? Or were Mom and Dad simply indulgent of their children's wants? I did not have any answers, but I surmised that it wasn't going to be easy understanding the American way. Neither would it be easy accepting or adjusting to American customs. I realized later that my difficulty was brought about by my cultural bias and naïveté. Given the situation, I expected my own familiar behavioral/cultural response. For instance, in the Philippines, as well as in many other Asian countries, children are rarely allowed, if at all, to "do their own thing" without the consent of their parents. Consultation with parents, older siblings, aunts and uncles, or grandparents is always sought. In America, I found out that from an early age, a person is encouraged to be independent, to make up his or her mind, and to stand up for his or her rights. Individualism is encouraged among the American youth, whereas among Asians, including Filipinos, group unity, togetherness, and harmony are valued.

Values such as obedience to authority (older people are vested with authority) and respect for elders are seriously observed and practiced. The young address their elders using terms of respect. Among the Tagalog, the particle *po* (sir, ma'am) or *opo* (yes sir, yes ma'am) is always used. Not to do so is considered rude. Children do not call anybody older by their first names. This deference to age contrasts sharply with the American notions of egalitarianism and informality.

American children, I observe, are allowed to call older people by their first names. I recall two interesting incidents, amusing now but definitely bothersome then. The first incident took place in the university cafeteria. To foster collegiality among the faculty and graduate students, professors and students usually ate lunch together. During one of these occasions, I heard a student greet a teacher, "Hey Bob! That was a tough exam! You really gave us a hard time, buddy!" I was stunned. I couldn't believe what I heard. All I could say to myself was, "My God! How bold and disrespectful!"

Not long afterward, I found myself in a similar scenario. This time, I was with some very young children of new acquaintances. They called to say hello and to ask if I could spend the weekend with the family. At their place, I met more people, young and not so young. Uninhibited, the children took the liberty of introducing me to everybody. Each child who played the role of "introducer" would address each person by his or her first name. No titles such as "Mr.," "Mrs.," or "Miss" were used; we were simply introduced as "Steve, this is Amparo" and "Amparo, this is Paula." Because I was not acquainted with the sociolinguistics of American communicative style, this took me quite by surprise. I was not prepared for the reality of being addressed as the children's equal. In my own experience, it took me some time to muster courage before I could call my senior colleagues by their first names.

A somewhat similar occurrence happened many years later. I had impressed on my little girl the proper and polite way to address older people, that is, for her always to say "Mr." or "Mrs." before mentioning their first names and family names. I used to prod and remind her often that it was the right thing to do. Imagine my surprise and embarrassment when one day I heard her greet our next-door neighbor saying "Hi Martha!" I asked her why she greeted her that way. She readily answered, "Mommy, Martha told me not to call her Mrs. _____ , just Martha!" What could I say? Since then, she was always called Martha, but I had qualms each time I heard my daughter greet her. In the Philippines, older people, regardless of their status in life, whether they are relatives or strangers, are always addressed using respectful terms such as *mang* (title for an elderly man), *iyo* (abbreviated variant for *tiyo*, or uncle, a title for a male relative but also used to address someone who is elderly), *aling* (respectful title for an older or elderly woman), and *manang* (a regional variant for *aling*). However, one gets used to doing things in a certain way after a while. So did I! After all, isn't that what adaptation is all about? But my cultural adventure or misadventure did not end here. This was only a prelude.

I was introduced into American culture from the periphery, which provided me with only a glimpse of the people's life-style, their passing moods and attitudes, and their values and ideas. I did not have the time, effort, or desire to take a long hard look at the cultural environment around me. I returned to the Philippines with some notions about American culture. If I have another chance, I told myself, I want to check it out judiciously and with objectivity. Seven years later, an opportunity presented itself. I was back in the "good old U.S.A.," this time to stay. I humored myself with the thought that I was smarter, wiser, and better prepared for challenges. I did not expect any serious problems. If there were problems, they would be inconsequential and therefore less stressful. This was far from the truth, however!

This time I was not alone against a whole new world. I had become a mother and was raising my child while virtually swimming against the current of cultural values that were not my own. True, there are clusters of universal human values to which everybody adheres. But it is likewise true that certain values are distinctive to a culture. Here lay the crux of an important problem that I needed to resolve. How was I going to bring up my child? Did I want her to grow up American, or did I want her to be a reflection and/or extension of myself, culturally speaking? The longer I pondered on these nagging questions, the more I began to realize that they were rather unfair questions. There were no easy answers.

There was, however, one thing of which I was certain: I wanted the best for my child, that is, the best of two worlds, America and my own. To do this, there were choices to be made. Predictably, I found myself straddling between two cultures, my right hand not knowing what my left hand was doing. At times, I found myself engaged in a balancing act in an effort to understand American culture without jeopardizing my cultural ways. Thus, alternatively, I would be strongly assertive and modestly defensive when my peculiar beliefs and actions were questioned.

Two incidents remain fresh in my mind. Briefly, someone made her observations very clearly to me by her remarks: "I see you always walk your daughter to and from school every day. . . . You know, many children in the neighborhood walk to school unaccompanied by adults. Why don't you let your daughter walk with them to school? She will learn to be on her own if you let go."

Another woman, some years later, asked me whether my daughter had started to drive, to which I answered "No." Surprised, she asked how my daughter could get around (to parties, movies, and so on). She remarked, "It would be easy for her and for you if she started taking driving lessons and got her own car." Forthright remarks! Fair criticism?

These two incidents bring into sharp focus the contrast between Filipino culture and American culture in the area of socialization. It is plain to see that in these instances, I am perceived as controlling and reprimanding, whereas the other person (American) is viewed as sociable, egalitarian, and indulgent. Because of the American emphasis on self-reliance and independence, relationships between the children and the (Asian) Filipino mother are often interpreted as overdependent. Mothers are often perceived as overprotective. This observation results from unfamiliarity with the traditional family dynamics of the (Asian) Filipino family. In order to avoid a distorted perception of one culture by another, it is extremely important that the uniqueness and cultural distinctiveness of a culture be explored, recognized, and respected for what it is. Otherwise, that which is not familiar, and therefore not clearly understood, would be viewed as "bizarre," although it is completely meaningful to members of another culture.

Among the Filipinos, life is governed by traditions that do not stress independence and autonomy of the individual. The family surpasses the individual. Hierarchical roles define each member's position in the network of relationships. These relationships are strictly prescribed, such as the relationship between children and parents, between father and children, and between mother and children. For instance, the mother plays a paramount role in the nurturance of the children. The burden of the child's well-being rests on the mother.

Going back to the heart of the problem—that is, the issue of childrearing values—I have made a conscious choice, and in doing so, my values, beliefs, and actions have been brought into question. I have reassured myself that there is no need to worry as long as my child benefits from the quality of life I have prayerfully sought and arduously worked for.

At this point, I come full circle to the question: How am I doing as a parent, as a mother? Did I do the right thing? Is my daughter growing up American? My answer would have to be: "It depends. Let's wait and see!"

NOTE

I wrote this article not to discredit or minimize the significance of American childrearing ideas, attitudes, and practices. I simply want to emphasize that there are cross-cultural differences in outlook, values, customs, and practices. Certainly, the socialization of the young is no exception.

SUGGESTED READINGS

McGOLDRICK, MONICA, JOHN PEARCE, AND JOSEPH GIORDANO, EDS.
1982   Ethnicity and Family Therapy. New York: Guilford Press.

MEAD, MARGARET, AND MARTHA WOLFENSTEIN, EDS.
1955   Childhood in Contemporary Cultures. Chicago: University of Chicago Press.

WHITING, BEATRICE B., AND CAROLYN P. EDWARDS
1988   Children of Different Worlds. Cambridge, MA: Harvard University Press.

⊜ Forms of Address: How Their Social Functions May Vary

SALIKOKO S. MUFWENE
The University of Chicago

Forms of address differ markedly in other countries. Professor Mufwene, raised in a French-speaking country in Africa, was brought up in a different, more formalized system. The American system of person-to-person address displays signs of informality, even in cases where the interactants have recently met. This was initially confusing to the author, and he perceived this informality as disrespectful, in comparison to the way he was raised. Whether using kinship terms of address, or terms for good friends or recent acquaintances, Americans do not distinguish between social relations.

Salikoko S. Mufwene *is native to Zaire (central Africa), where he lived until he came to the United States to attend graduate school in 1974 at the University of Chicago. He received his Ph.D. in Linguistics in 1979. Since then, he has taught at the University of the West Indies, Jamaica, and at the University of Georgia. He has recently accepted the post of professor of Linguistics at the University of Chicago. His research interests include semantics and syntax, language and culture, and pidgin and creole speech.*

The point of view presented in this essay is primarily Bantu, one of the several groups of sub-Saharan Africans typically characterized as black. Moreover, the outlook is that of a person who grew up in the transition from colonial Zaire (then the Belgian Congo, in central Africa) to postindependence Zaire, in an education system that fosters an interesting coexistence of colonial European and local African cultures. From a sociolinguistic point of view, French, inherited from the colonial days as the official language and the medium of education from the fourth grade up to higher education, has been adapted to convey this marriage of African and colonial European cultures heavily anchored in the African tradition.

In this essay, I show how this background affected my reaction over fifteen years ago to English forms of address, as used at a major midwestern American university. With time, I have also learned that the customs described in this essay do not apply universally to the overall American society. However, I think that these first impressions reflect best my then unaccultured perception of a facet of American culture.

The term "form of address" is used in this essay as much for names, like *Peter, Mary,* and *Bob,* as for titles, like *Mr., Mrs., Dr.,* and *Professor,* which are normally used before last or full names, for example, *Mr. (Paul) Simon* or *Dr. (Alice) Rosenfeld.* The term is also used for other titles such as *sir* and *ma'am,* normally used without a name; for kinship terms such as *Dad, Mom,* and *son* used to address relatives; for pet names such as *buttercup* and *cupcake;* or for any word used to address a person. Ethnographically, these forms of address specify the relation between the speaker and the addressee (for example, pals, professionals, parent-child, lovers) and the terms of their interaction (for example, distant, close, intimate), depending sometimes on the specific circumstances of the communication. To take an American example, a person named *Alice Rosenfeld* may be addressed in various ways, depending on context. She may be addressed as *Dr. Rosenfeld* in formal professional interaction, as *Mrs.* or *Ms. Rosenfeld* in situations where she is not well known, as *Mom* by her children, as *Alice* by her husband and colleagues in places where professional relations are not formal, and as *dear, darling,* or *honey* by her husband in intimate interaction.

I will restrict my observations on the American system to the usage of forms of address after the first time people have been introduced to each other. I will ignore those situations where preestablished relationships might allow usage of pet names and kinship titles, for instance, the title *uncle* extended to friends of the speaker's parents or blood uncles. However, it will help to provide more general background information about myself at this point, so that the reader may understand my original shock at how Americans address each other, at least at the university I attended.

In my Bantu background, addressees' names are often avoided in quite a variety of situations in order to express deference and/or intimacy. For instance, in the Bantu vernacular languages, people of the same age as one's parents are addressed by the same titles as the parents of the same sex, with the terms *papa* or *tata* (father) or *mama* (mother) prefixed to their names to express deference, for example, *Papa Kaniki* or *Mama Moseka.* These honorifics (that is, special forms of address for respect) are also used alone, without a name, to express both deference and intimacy when the speaker knows the addressee closely. For instance, in Kikongo-Kituba (my regional lingua franca), a close relation of the speaker's family who is of approximately the same age as, or older than, his or her father may be addressed as follows: *Papa, ebwe?* (Papa, how are you?)

When used alone to address strangers, the honorifics *papa* and *mama* are simple markers of politeness corresponding to the English honorifics *sir* and *ma'am*, used without a name, or to the honorifics *Mr., Mrs., Ms., Dr.,* and the like prefixed to the last names in formal interaction. These honorifics also are often used for addressees of the age group of the speaker's children as affective forms of address, corresponding to, for instance, the use of *son* by a nonkin. Thus, the sentence *Papa, ebwe?* used by an adult to a child is affective and may be translated idiomatically as "How are you, son/darling/dear?" All these Bantu forms of address fit in a system in which addressees' names are generally avoided, a practice to which I return below.

People of the age group of the speaker's older siblings are addressed in Kikongo-Kituba either by prefixing the kinship honorific *yaya* (older sibling) to their names for deference or by using the title alone for both deference and intimacy, for example, *Yaya Kalala*. Ethnographically, this corresponds in American English to addressing such a close relation by his or her first name or nickname.

A number of older male persons are assimilated to uncles and are addressed on the same pattern as above with the kinship honorific *noko* (uncle), for example, *Noko Mukoko*. However, note that many of the people addressed with this honorific would not be addressed with the honorific *uncle* in American English, since they may not be close friends of the speaker's parents or blood uncles.

Adult close friends often address one another by their professional titles, if these are considered as achievements (for example, *Munganga ebwe?* [Dr. (MD), how are you?]), or by their nicknames or play names (for example, *Mbongo mpasi, ebwe?* [Hard Money, how are you?]). This custom is to express intimacy. In the case of professional titles, close associates bear the responsibility of setting up examples for others to follow; deference starts at home. Once more, usage of addressees' names is generally restricted to situations where it is absolutely necessary to make clear which person is being addressed, for instance, when more than one person in the same setting may be addressed by the same honorific.

Much of the same behavior is carried on in local French, except that the honorifics *monsieur* (sir), *madame* (ma'am), and *mademoiselle* (Miss) are generally substituted for the traditional honorifics derived from kin terms. More recently, the honorifics *citoyen* (male citizen) and *citoyenne* (female citizen) were used by a political-ideological decree from the government in 1971 to distinguish the natives from foreigners.[1] Like the Bantu honorifics based on kin terms, they are generally used alone without the addressees' names. In all such cases, it is generally thought that only deference, not social distance, is expressed. Thus, translations with western European honorifics generally distort the ethnographic meaning somewhat, since they suggest social distance where none is suggested in either the Bantu forms of address with honorifics for deference or the local French adaptations to the system. For instance, the translation of the local French sentence *Suivez-moi, citoyen(ne)* (Follow me, citoyen(ne)) either becomes odd if *citoyen(ne)* is also translated as *citizen* or distorted if it is translated idiomatically as *sir* or *ma'am*. In the latter case, the idiomatic translation assigns higher status to the addressee, whereas the honorific *citoyen(ne)* does not.

Last, aside from the fact that names are generally avoided, it matters little in the Bantu system whether the first name or the surname is used. In any case, to make up for the tradition, speakers of local French often use the traditional Bantu honorifics, the kind of thing that is done less comfortably in a native French setting, unless all the interactants are from the same Bantu background. Note also that, as a rule, French requires that the polite pronoun *vous*, rather than the intimate pronoun *tu*, be used to address people concomitantly with the above titles. In fact, *vous* in the construction *Vous pouvez partir, monsieur/madame* (You may leave, sir/ma'am) assigns high status to the addressee. Using the traditional Bantu honorifics makes allowance for the intimate or status-free pronoun *tu*, which in a construction such as *Tu peux partir, papa* (You may leave, father) conveys both deference and intimacy or lack of status, depending on the case. Using *vous* together with *papa* makes explicit either the higher status of the addressee or the speaker's decision to establish social distance in the interaction.

In my American experience, I had to learn new norms of conduct. Honorifics based on age, and often even on rank, are commonly avoided.[2] My shock started in my first class, when the professor asked to be addressed as Jerry. Most of the other professors did likewise, regardless of age.[3] I found out that generally people do not give their titles when introducing themselves. More often than not, they either give only the first name or ask to be addressed by the first name. Further, the first names have usually been clipped to monosyllabics or disyllabics; for example, *Fred* is short for *Frederick* and *Ed* is short for *Edward*. Sometimes first names have been replaced by seemingly unrelated short nicknames; for example, *Bob* and *Bobby* are short for *Robert* and *Ted* is short for *Edward*. The native French transitional address system according to which persons are addressed by their honorifics and the pronoun *vous*, until there is a tacit or explicit agreement to convert to an intimate and informal mode of address, does not exist in America.

There is more to this American system of address. Foreigners are rebaptized, so to speak! The often long and "complicated" first names are replaced by nicknames. Ever since my first class, I have usually been addressed as *Sali*. The few Americans that say "Salikoko" either find the name "musical" or want to show off their familiarity with foreign names, in contrast with the regular reaction "I can't say that one."

However, addressing people by their first names does not necessarily mean a close relationship or intimacy. As suggested above, there are ways of expressing closeness or intimacy, but these will not be discussed here. The American system of address is basically a sign of informality, which is created from the onset of a social relationship, much sooner than I would have expected in the mixed cultural background I came from.

I also learned something else about names. As noted above, it makes little difference in the Bantu system whether one is addressed by one's first name or by one's surname, whenever names must or can be used. Names are typically avoided when addressing some relations, such as close friends, and names are taboo in addressing or referring to one's own parents. In the case of friends, professional titles or descriptive nicknames dealing with events in one's life are normally used. Name avoidance is a sign of closeness or intimacy. It is considered disrespectful to address ascending and descending in-laws by their names. Their kinship titles must be used not only to express deference but also to reassert the close social bond of the extended family by marriage. The expectation to use kinship honorifics in this case applies even to spouses' relatives when they interact among themselves, for instance, when the wife's cousin interacts with the husband's cousin.

The Bantu custom is in sharp contrast with the American custom of using first names or nicknames between close friends and with most in-laws.[4] In the beginning, I found it bizarre to see ascending and descending in-laws (fathers- and mothers-in-law and sons- and daughters-in-law, respectively) address each other by their first names and to see them interact casually with each other. (In my background, ascending and descending in-laws maintain avoidance relationships.) The new custom gave me the impression that Americans did not care much about these special, affined ties and that all social relations were of the same kind. I also assumed then that Americans did not distinguish between acquaintances and friends. In addition, I thought that Americans became personal with people they had just met rather quickly. (This impression was due essentially to the stereotypical French address system I had learned in school in Zaire.) As noted above, acculturation to American ways has now taken the original shock away. However, coming from my Third World background, there was more to be overwhelmed by than space-age technology.

ACKNOWLEDGMENTS

I am grateful to James Armstrong, Kathleen MacQueen, and Jennifer Eason for feedback on drafts of this essay. I alone assume full responsibility for its shortcomings.

NOTES

1. This custom was patterned on the French system during Napoleon Bonaparte's regime in the nineteenth century to suggest an egalitarian revolution in the way Zaireans interact with each other. The corruption and the socioeconomic discriminatory system it was meant to eradicate have grown stronger, starting from the political leadership, and a reactionary trend has now reverted to the current French forms of address with *monsieur* (sir), *madame* (ma'am), or *mademoiselle* (miss) when formality is required.

2. I will disregard here professional titles such as *Dr.* (for medical doctors) that act as part of the name in professional settings. Constraints are more complex here regarding when the title may be dropped.

3. There are apparently some exceptions to this observation. In my graduate school experience, I knew of some professors in their sixties that most students addressed as Mr. _____ , though their much younger colleagues still addressed them by their first names.

4. I do not wish to ignore cases of assimilation where in-laws are addressed by the same kinship titles the spouse uses for them. However, coming from my background, another peculiarity here is that the assimilation applies almost only to the speaker relative to his or her spouse's relatives; his or her own relatives do not assimilate and show intimacy or closeness by using first names.

NINE

First Impressions: Diary of a French Anthropologist in New York City

FRANCOISE DUSSART
University of Connecticut

Moving from the solitude of the Australian Outback, where she had been studying Australian aboriginal culture, a French anthropologist finds herself living in New York City in a multiethnic neighborhood characterized by poverty, homelessness, and drug dealing. From reflections of seven months, excerpted from her diary, she not only describes the neighborhood, the apartment complex, and some of its residents but also comments on some aspects of the culture of the neighboring, wealthier residents of "The City."

Françoise Dussart *was raised in France, Africa, England, and the United States. She received her B.A. and Masters in Anthropology from the Sorbonne University in Paris (1980, 1982) and her Ph.D. in Anthropology from the Australian National University at Canberra (1989). Professor Dussart is an assistant professor of Anthropology at the University of Connecticut at Storrs.*

Anthropologists are, by nature, note-takers. What follows are slightly neatened excerpts from the diary I kept when I first reached New York City in the fall of 1988.

ARRIVAL

The plane will be touching down soon. After five years of working in an Australian aboriginal community, I suspect I am prepared to handle the "exoticism" of New York. How much stranger can the ceremonies of Manhattanites be than those of the Warlpiri Aborigines? Certainly the system of kinship will be a lot easier to handle. Here you do not have to marry your mother's mother's brother's daughter's daughter. I will try to suspend judgment. But is that possible?

The plane banks over New York. I have to stop thinking of the city's geography in terms of aboriginal culture. I look out the plane's oval window and, seeing the sparkling skyline, recall the fires burning in the central Australian desert. This kind of obsessive comparison making is the observer's kiss of death. Still, the temptation is always there.

On landing, I am confronted by more differences. Stopped by an immigration official, I am asked to prove that I have adequate funds for my stay in the United States, and then I am questioned about my profession. I respond in the most general terms that, "anthropology is the study of people, their history, their habits, and their rituals." The official seems satisfied with my answers. I have money and a profession, the twinned necessities of American acceptance. (I guess that's why they call the man at the airport a custom's official!) Back in Yuendumu, the settlement at which I conducted my fieldwork, those questions would have had little meaning. Arrival would have been marked by a long and involved interrogation about my family genealogy.

The ride into Manhattan is marked by general discussion of "The City," as if there is no other city in the world. In this regard, residents of Manhattan seem particularly geocentric. (I am taught over time the specialized lexicon of the region. Brooklyn, the Bronx, and other boroughs are part of New York City but are never referred to as "The City," a term restricted to the borough of Manhattan.)

I am told what I should do ("The museums are nice, and the art galleries are fantastic") and what I should not do (a much longer list that includes not going to Harlem alone, avoiding confrontation, and carrying enough money to satisfy muggers, robbers, and other petty criminals).

Two words linger in my head as we snake through the traffic into New York: danger and inequity. The danger arises from all the talk of robbery, burglary, and rape. I am told to fear the city before I've even had a chance to explore it. The inequity arises from the scenes outside the window: the shelterless populations next to neatly kept homes. These two words figure into the storytelling tradition of the city's residents. Real estate and crime are the subject of many conversations. Perhaps this is the modern-day legacy of the fireside storytellers of central Europe.

FIRST DAY

I will be staying in the very part of town I was told to avoid: the southern tip of Harlem. As I walk around the neighborhood (the environs of West 107th Street), I am confronted by the speed with which the affluence of neighborhoods changes. From one block to the next, you can switch from doorman apartments to tenements populated by people of predominantly Central American origin. My accommodations are found in the second form of habitation.

The rectilinearity of Manhattan is an impressive quality of this city. All the streets are on a grid that denies natural geography. Local residents do not understand notions of uphill and downhill. Their awareness of which way is north or south is based on the numbering of the streets, not on any geographical sense of the terrain. This is so unlike aboriginal culture, where location is defined by terrain. (The urge to compare, I guess, is inevitable.) "Go to the water hole and walk east until the mulga trees area" is replaced by the simplicities of consecutive numbering (though I am told that lower Manhattan rejects the grid completely).

Even before I arrive, I am told of the drug addicts and mentally disabled homeless who walk the streets. In my new neighborhood, I discover that the homeless situation is quite depressing. Unwed mothers with children also make up a part of this migrant army of despair. The scenes remind me of the "Courtyard of Miracles" in the French novel *Notre Dame de Paris,* but we are not in the sixteenth century. How can it be that such a rich city has so many beggars? Perhaps that is why it is so rich.

I have already started to notice that different ethnic groups dominate different street activities. It is obvious that the Koreans run the fruit stores on Broadway. There are also other groups overseeing specialized markets. A small group of South American Indians sells flowers out of shopping carts they roll around the West Side of Manhattan. One Peruvian woman sells native sweaters and dolls from the inside of a heated car. Dozens of impoverished black men sell castaway clothing, books, shoes, lamps, and junk salvaged from the garbage of wealthier locals. Even in junk selling there are differences to be observed. The better-off vendor uses a table and has prices marked with little stickers, whereas the more desperate street people line up their wares on the cement and take pretty much what is offered. The homeless tend to avoid corners because corners are too windy, and their clothing is ragged at best. The slightly more upscale salesperson, on the other hand, will gladly set up a stand on a corner.

I observe more links between ethnicity and occupation. Most of the taxi drivers in New York seem to be Haitian. A driver named Jean Jean from Port au Prince describes the difference between being a cabbie in Haiti and being a cabbie in New York. "The passengers are much more trusting in Haiti," he tells me in French. He says that New York passengers, fearful of being overcharged, almost always provide detailed instructions of exactly what route they wish to take. I let him choose the path he wishes, all the time trying to test myself on the orientation of east, west, north, and south.

FIRST WEEK

I have settled in the top-floor apartment of a five-story walk-up on the Upper West Side of Manhattan, just south of Columbia University. The university's presence is not felt. This is a Spanish-speaking world. Most of the residents come from Central and South America. The food, the smells, the language, and the way in which life is played out on the streets are all wholly Latino.

The rent in the apartment where I am staying is low, and this fact dominates much of the conversation I have with native New Yorkers. Sometimes I feel that real estate and safety are the only two topics of conversation. Safety is discussed because a number of nonminority ac-quaintances are made nervous by the "unsafe" nature of my new neigh-borhood. When I ask what constitutes "unsafe," they seem to associate predominantly white neighborhoods with protective environments, even though they admit to having been confronted in those areas as well.

Back at my apartment building, I ask a Puerto Rican neighbor (as best as I can without speaking Spanish) where he feels safe. He points to our building. Safety, clearly, is relative. In this "dangerous" neighborhood, he can buy food, pitch pennies, and go to church. He says he would never go to Brooklyn.

I could picture a map of New York City with "safe" areas shaded in by different ethnic groups. I suspect that the whole of the city would be covered. Likewise, "unsafe" shading would produce similar results.

SECOND WEEK

I have been spending my time trying to map out the cultural geography of my neighborhood. Never have economic discrepancies been so dramatically defined. Stepping out of my building, I am surrounded by a Spanish ghetto with all the cover-story problems (crack, unwed mothers, welfare dependency), but walking west just half a block brings me to a solidly middle-class row of cooperative apartments, and just another hundred yards more brings on distinctly wealthy residents. In a three-minute walk, I have moved from poverty to Crabtree & Evelyn, a fancy goods store specializing in luxury soaps. I am told that if I were to move east from my building entrance (to Columbus Avenue), I would find myself among the notorious crack dens of the city. I have not yet walked on that avenue.

I can't think of a European city in which wealth and poverty exist in such close proximity. There are, of course, ethnic distinctions to be made. When I note "poor," it is a poor Hispanic and black population, and when I write "rich," it is predominantly white, though Japanese investment has made its presence felt here, too. (The buzzers on every other door of the co-ops along Riverside Drive have signs written in *Kanji*.)

I have started asking some of the older residents (often a gold mine for the fieldworker) about the evolution of the neighborhood. I learn that until the late 1960s this was a predominantly Irish neighborhood. It is hard to believe that all traces of that presence have been eradicated. After strolling around, I find one last defiant marker of that Irish legacy: the Kennedy Funeral Home. (I guess it's appropriate that the last establishment to stay deals in the dead and dying.) The establishment stands out. It has a faux-Cape house facade with white embroidered curtains. The owner is still a Mr. Kennedy, but he has hired a Hispanic consultant to maintain ties to the community.

I have been feeling many of the same frustrations in New York that I had during the first few months of fieldwork in Australia because I cannot speak the language of the streets. I keep thinking about the halting conversation I had earlier in the week with my Puerto Rican neighbor, Tony. He has an English vocabulary of perhaps fifty words. English does not get one very far in the *bodegas* and *carnecerias* that dot Amsterdam Avenue.

Fluency in the neighborhood is generationally distinguishable. The younger population speaks English and Spanish fluently, so I converse with them. But for Tony and other first-generation immigrants, communication with English-speakers is almost all gesture. Once in a while whites need to talk to the superintendent, whose command of English is practically nonexistent. Usually one of his children comes to help everyone reach some kind of understanding.

A typical view from my window includes clutches of young women (girls, really) tending to babies, the heads of older women poking out of windows, and men on the street pitching pennies, fixing unfixable cars, and drinking beer out of green bottles or rum from a shared brown bag. It is rare to see groups of men and women together.

THIRD WEEK

I went to a number of social events this week. As usual, everyone at the gathering was, like me, white and middle class. I was amazed how tight a network of friendships and professional links emerged during the meal. I have clearly stumbled into the American equivalent of the French intellectual elite. The same schools, the same vacation spots, and the same books are constantly mentioned. There are differences, however. French intellectual life is played out on a more intimate scale, so that in France the country's top lawyers, actors, writers, and filmmakers often intersect at various social events. That is not the case here in New York. There are book parties for writers, museum openings for art critics and artists, and movie screenings for specialists in cinema. Of course I am moving in a slightly less stylish circle, but the point remains that there is a professional and ethnic homogeneity in the social gatherings I have attended.

I must now add another topic of obsession to the list that previously included only real estate and security. The obsession surfaces in the question asked before all others and pursued with the greatest intensity: What do you do? It seems that acquaintances need to know the nature of your professional life in order to feel at ease. In France it would be considered rude to initiate a conversation on such a topic. Conversations in France are introduced by discussions of family origins. White Americans seem less concerned by such genealogical inquiries.

I had an interesting conversation with a group of five women all roughly my age. I say "interesting" not because there were any overlapping interests but because I felt so alien. Most of the discussion centered around their bodies. I was amazed to find them absolutely at ease discussing their weight, how much they were going to lose, and how they were going to lose it. There was a detailed conversation on the relative merits of aerobics, swimming, and tennis, all activities that had as their goal weight loss. I wrote to a friend of mine in France about the discussion, and in the correspondence that followed we agreed that such intimacies would never be revealed in such a setting. Talk about the imperfections of one's body is limited to closest friends and mothers.

The commitment to keeping fit is visible everywhere in the neighborhood outside the Spanish community where I live. Athletic supply stores can be found every few blocks, and the reservoir a mile from my building is regularly circled by joggers in various states of fitness (I once saw a father jogging while pushing a baby carriage).

Although the American women I talked with are comfortable talking about the physical condition of their bodies, discussions of sensual condition are taboo. Again, comparison with the French experience is inevitable, where strangers are perfectly comfortable talking about the satisfaction and the limitation of their sexual liaisons. Maybe such discussion makes my American women friends uncomfortable because it suggests prefeminist roles. I know that my more traditional "feminine" interests such as cooking and knitting have frequently gotten me into trouble with professional women who find such activities frivolous and counterproductive.

These last few weeks in New York recalled the first lecture I had in cultural anthropology. The professor stressed the need to avoid cultural relativity that denies the uniqueness of the community under investigation. The more I learn about New York, the less comfortable I become with the terms and conclusions I have made. I suspect that if I gave the community in which I live the same attention I applied to the Warlpiri Aborigines, it would take many years to find answers to the questions that constantly confront me. What is the relationship between "black-magic candles" sold at the Haitian botanica and the Catholic religious figures? Why do my neighbors play the illegal numbers games on the street that pay much lower dividends than the state-sanctioned lotteries? But on a more theoretical level, I would like to know how much this Hispanic community adopts the values of white America, how it resists assimilation, and how it adapts elements of the society that surrounds it. Each question provokes twenty more questions.

FIRST MONTH

I gave my first dinner party. I was fascinated to see what people brought in the way of gifts: two bottles of wine, a dessert, and even a head of broccoli the guest thought I might want to toss into the salad. Each of these gifts, different as they are, share one common element—consumption during the meal. In France, such gift giving would be considered somehow inappropriate. Flowers are the most common offering to the host or hostess.

A few guests expressed surprise that I actually cooked the meal instead of ordering from a restaurant or preparing some microwaved delicacies. When I asked them if they ever cooked, they said proudly that they had never turned on their oven (they had been living in the same apartment for the last three years). After the party I had expected some reciprocal invitations, but none came. When I asked why the party was received so unilaterally, I discovered that many New Yorkers are reluctant to reveal where they live. The reasons are complex and diverse. One fellow I spoke to admitted he was embarrassed by the size of his apartment: It was too small a space in which to entertain. Another woman made a point never to invite anybody to her apartment. "It is my sanctuary," she said, "why would I reveal it to anyone?"

Subsequent dinners with these acquaintances were held at restaurants (except once in the home of close friends). The guests, each on separate occasions, called me up and proposed that we get together again with other friends in a restaurant. The effort of getting together for a meal at a restaurant is one facet of New York hospitality among people in their twenties and early thirties. But we often all share the bill!

SECOND MONTH

I attend my first women's studies seminar at a New York university. I have no idea what to expect and so arrive early to gather my thoughts. The participants start to enter, and I quickly realize that no men will be attending. The mood is warm and supportive, with a lot of high-pitched salutation and kissing. The seminar starts, and the speaker begins her lecture on "The Roles of German Jewish Women During the Second World War." The woman next to me shakes her head while the paper is being delivered. Another woman sucks her tooth, and still a third objects out loud. When the lecture is over, the listeners begin an open assault on her ideas, challenging not only her data but her premises as well. I am surprised by the vehemence of these condemnations. In seminars I attended in Britain and Australia, I never saw anger and argumentation. In France, where the pleasures of disputations are legendary, such a conflict would have been the start of a long-standing feud. That's not what happened here in New York. The seminar ended, smiles returned to the faces of the participants and the lecturer, and the women kissed one another good-bye.

THIRD MONTH

Although the poverty is sometimes unnerving, I am constantly surprised by the intensity of community spirit among people in the neighborhood. Most of middle-class Manhattan exists on the nuclear family level, while West 107th Street is always displaying the entanglements, jealousies, and affections of the extended family. I have very little to do with these interactions, but increasingly the residents are recognizing that my stay may not be temporary. The triumphs of neighborliness are small ones. Yesterday, Tony helped me carry a heavy shopping bag to the front door of my fifth-floor apartment.

FOURTH MONTH

The temperature has dropped well below freezing. The men who linger on the street corner have retreated into cars they keep heated, into the lobby of the nearby funeral home, into grocery stores, and into basements that reveal the glow of old color TVs. Bottles of rum are generally passed around.

There is clearly a generational separation in the male population. Rum is not an adequate stimulant for the younger men of the community. I regularly walk over the tiny plastic envelopes in which crack is sold. The dealing can be observed from my living room window. The transaction itself is a complex pirouette marked by dropoffs, cash exchanges, coded negotiations, and the ultimate sale.

One young entrepreneur has hung a pair of shoes over a lamppost. This marker is to alert out-of-town drug buyers to the availability of his wares. The cars stop, and after brief discussion he pulls the little plastic bag from his sock.

Missing from the street life are the women. They can be seen at the windows of their kitchens throughout the neighborhood. The apartment two floors below, which is occupied by the family of the building's superintendent, has no fewer than four generations of women coming and going. Disposable diapers, baby carriages, and small children are carried up and down the staircase. Women spend most of their time in kitchens with their children and female friends and relatives. Each sex relies on the emotional support of their friends and relatives of the same sex and the same generation level.

FIFTH MONTH

I spend the day taking a casual survey of the building's thirteen apartments. The ground-floor apartment is occupied by three Columbia college students with a serious commitment to hard-rock music. There is a sort of music war that takes place between Led Zeppelin and the Latino tunes. The second floor is occupied by a young, low-paid editor at a publishing house and a family from the Dominican Republic living in two apartments. The nature of this family must be defined in the anthropological literature as matrifocal. The third floor has an extended family from Ecuador, another one from Cuba, and three brothers from Puerto Rico. The fourth floor is occupied by a white American actor, a nuclear family of jazz musicians, and an extended family from Bolivia. The fifth floor is occupied by three Puerto Ricans, a white student from Columbia University, a free-lance journalist, and a cultural anthropologist. One apartment is empty now. It used to be a "crack house," as white people refer to it here. One morning, the police raided the apartment. The only objects left in the apartment are a sword and Latino American saints, the heads and bodies lying separately on the floor. Maybe the police pulled the statues apart because they thought that the drug dealers were hiding the white powder inside them.

SIXTH MONTH

The windows of my office look out on a Spanish funeral home. Quite often I see grieving women. They scream, roll in the street, and sob uncontrollably. They show their grief to the entire community. The men tend to be less demonstrative. Once the coffin is brought out of the funeral home, it is quickly taken away. Death is not allowed to linger in New York. When a woman in a building adjacent to mine committed suicide by jumping off the roof, her body was taken away by the police less than fifteen minutes later. I am amazed to discover that there is no place to be buried in Manhattan.

There are two churches on 107th Street. One is a Catholic church, which is the most popular, and the second is called the Kingdom Hall of the Jehovah's Witnesses. Proportionally, white people attend the Pentecostal services more than the Catholic services, though they represent a small proportion of the people who attend services in both places. White people go elsewhere.

People cross themselves as they pass the statue of Jesus Christ that stands outside the Catholic church. Often, several coins lie at the feet of the statue, and they are later picked up by homeless people. I have seen this done in Italy or Spain and even in some parts of rural France. But people's religious habits are not so simply defined and limited. In fact, within a few yards both from the church and from the Kingdom Hall, there is a strange store in which they sell all kinds of natural or health food and all the necessary apparatuses for magico-religious practices as performed in parts of Latin and South America and the West Indies. Their collection of objects and of statues of saints (like those lying on the floor across the hall from me) is impressive. There, one can also buy candles to keep black cats away or to charm a lover. The Korean grocery store had to adapt, and they are now selling spray cans against black cats (considered bad luck among the Spanish-speaking people).

SEVENTH MONTH

It is much warmer outside. The men both young and old are back in the streets rolling dice, listening to loud music, fixing cars, and selling drugs. The women in the community emerge briefly in the late afternoon to join in the streetside discussions. Chairs and even a couch have been put on the sidewalk in anticipation of summer.

I am amazed by the variety of street games that are played by the older men. They can pitch pennies and roll dice for hours at a stretch. (Dice are played when the men of the street are cash rich; pennies are pitched when they are poor.) Occasionally a checkerboard or sets of dominoes will make a brief appearance. There is one man—the fellow who brought out the couch—who comes every day and calls out for mates to play with him—to play for money, of course. He seems to live off his winnings from the games. The only time of the week he cannot be found is on Sunday when he attends mass.

The increase in temperature marks a switch from rum drinking to beer drinking. The men in the neighborhood have a strong preference for Heineken, and though none of the men is rich, the bottles are never returned for deposit. Monday mornings are marked by dozens of empty brown bags littering the sidewalk. When the men are low on money, they pitch pennies and drink Budweiser.

The bottles are usually picked up by the neighborhood Hispanic homeless man named Junior. The people who live here also give him food, drinks, and money. One of the superintendents has given him access to a basement so that he and his dog can seek shelter for the night.

Once in a while, often under the influence of crack or heroin, he becomes violent and insults some of the men who look after him. The victims usually ignore him and to get rid of him give him money or a beer. Here people take care of their "mads" and drug users.

Each time I try to characterize the community in which I now live, I am struck by the diversity within what is often perceived to be Latino cultures. I am referred to by the Spanish-speaking people on 107th Street as one of *los Americanos;* they do not even know that I am French.

I live in a building not of Hispanics but of Bolivians, Ecuadorians, Dominicans, Puerto Ricans, and Cubans. They are not fully integrated in the larger American society, and they are not fully integrated in their homeland either. They seem to be very aware of what is happening in their respective countries through radio programs, television, news that new migrants bring with them, and visits home every two years or so. They seem to construct their identities in relation to both environments, here and there, and so construct a unique environment that includes other cultural groups they may never have met in other circumstances.

The tendency to judge must still be fought. I still make comparisons, but less often.

REFERENCES

BANTON, M.

1983   Racial and Ethnic Competition. Cambridge: Cambridge University Press.

BASTIDE, R.

1966   Les Ameriques Noires. Paris: PBP, Payot.

BOURDIEU, P.

1979   La Distinction. Paris: Les Editions de Minuit.

HALL, S.

1985   Religious Ideologies and Social Movements in Jamaica. In Religion and Ideology. R. Bocock and K. Thompson, eds. Manchester: Manchester University.

LÉVI-STRAUSS, C.

1961   A World on the Wane. New York: Criterion Books.
(1955)

Life and Cultures: The Test of Real Participant Observation

E. L. CERRONI-LONG
Eastern Michigan University

Studying other cultures from afar, from books and in the classroom, should prepare one for the contrastive principles of living in a new culture. However, when Professor Cerroni-Long, an Asian scholar from Italy, visited Japan, she discovered that intellectual preparation does not protect one from culture shock. For her, the need to understand, to lend predictability to the cross-cultural encounter became a necessity for mental equilibrium. The conscious application of cultural anthropological techniques provided her with the foundations for both survival and understanding.

    From having earned a Ph.D. in Anthropology at an American university, in combination with her experiences in many other cultural settings, Professor Cerroni-Long is able to explore some American culture patterns from an entirely different perspective.

E. L. Cerroni-Long *is an associate professor of Anthropology at Eastern Michigan University, in Ypsilanti. She was born and raised in Italy, where she received a Doctorate in Oriental Studies from the University of Venice (1970). She was a postdoctoral student at the University of Kyoto, Japan, from 1970 to 1972. She received a Ph.D. in Anthropology from UCLA in 1986. Dr. Cerroni-Long specializes in the study of intercultural relations and in the last twenty years has conducted research in various areas of Europe, Asia, and North America.*

One of the students in my field methods class—slightly exasperated by the seeming intricacies of the ethnographic enterprise—said it best: "It's easy for you to be an anthropologist! . . . You are a *foreigner!*"

Indeed, I have been a foreigner much of my life, and I consider myself a "professional stranger," not just because of my disciplinary specialization but truly as a result of life experiences that came about quite fortuitously but that I think have contributed in a crucial way to the depth of my anthropological perspective.

Growing up in northern Italy, in a family of artists and scholars passionately dedicated to the study of Italian intellectual traditions, I had a limited experience of "foreignness." Italy is an ethnically homogeneous society, poor enough not to attract—until recently—any sizable groups of immigrants from abroad and bourgeois enough to create extremely effective regional and occupational cleavages, so that differences in behavior are seldom experienced within one's own social circle. When differences do arise, they can be easily explained away. Actually, my own extended family harbored sharp regional differences—with my father's side being committedly Roman, my mother's side just as adamantly Friulian, and various other members having allegiances to the Venician region in which we lived. But I always attributed the continuous conflict in styles of behavior to personality factors or simply to the tiresome unpredictability of grown-ups, and I spent little time analyzing it. I was too busy dreaming of faraway times and places—Asia, ancient Arabia, Africa—places I had never visited but with which I felt a great affinity, possibly having been inspired by family lore of glorious colonial experiences in Libya, by the exotic Northern African heirlooms I played with as a child, or by the intangible but very real "Oriental" flavor one can still find in Venician architecture, art, history, and traditions.

Also, coming of age in the heady 1960s, when the West was enthusiastically rediscovering the "wisdom of the East," I could strengthen my interest in Eastern civilizations with a growing appreciation for their aesthetic and spiritual expressions. I can now see that my love for Zen Buddhism was stimulated by the prose of Alan Watts, my understanding of Islamic civilization was built on Burton's and Lawrence's descriptions, and my fascination with Indian thought was heavily dependent on Eliade's popularizations. My interest in Eastern civilizations was genuine, and when the time came to choose a graduate program of study, I was very excited to enter the newly created "Oriental Institute" of the University of Venice. Here I spent several blissful years exploring all sorts of arcane areas of knowledge, with the freedom of choice and the instructional guidance that are the mark of truly outstanding academic programs. As time went by, I restricted my interest to the "Buddhist area" of Asian civilization, and later I decided to specialize in Japanese studies, writing a dissertation on the relationship between certain aspects of contemporary Japanese literature and the Japanese philosophical tradition. When I obtained my doctorate, in 1970, I felt I was quite knowledgeable about Japan, and when I received a two-year research scholarship to be pursued at the University of Kyoto I left Italy without the slightest doubt about my ability to adjust easily to my research setting and to work on my project—the analysis of Japanese social change through literary expressions—easily and successfully.

DISCOVERING ANTHROPOLOGY

It took all of three days in Japan, the time necessary for me to make my way to the foreign researchers' dormitory to which my sponsors had assigned me, to change my outlook in a most dramatic way. My excitement about exploring "the Orient" started to dim by the time the plane landed at the Hong Kong airport, on its last stopover before reaching Japan. I had been flying for many hours and tiredness was certainly affecting me, but I remember looking around the transit lounge and having the distinct feeling of being on a different planet. It was not just that the physical appearance of the majority of the people surrounding me was so markedly different from what I was used to, it was also that they acted so strange! To begin with, so many people were squatting down—rather than sitting or standing—that I automatically scrutinized the floor to see if they were looking for something. Also, it disturbed my sense of propriety that so many people had taken off their shoes or were wearing them as if they were sandals, their feet halfway in and with the heels flattened out. Above all, though, I could not shake the feeling that people's gestures, their facial expressions, the interpersonal distances they kept, and the overall noise level their interactions created were somehow "all wrong."

Things did not get any better when I finally arrived in Japan and spent a short orientation period in Tokyo before proceeding toward my assigned destination, Kyoto. The fact that people seemed to have the greatest difficulty in understanding what I thought was fluent Japanese puzzled and irritated me—I discovered only much later that I was using linguistic expressions as obsolete as Chaucerian English. But what I kept finding most disturbing was the general noise level characterizing public places, the size and density of the crowds, and the frequency with which people waiting for a bus, using a public phone, or simply hanging out would adopt a squatting position.

By the time I finally made it to my room in Kyoto, exhausted by the long trip and in the grip of what I later came to recognize as a classic case of severe culture shock, I was determined never to leave it again, unless it was to go to the nearest airport, homeward bound. Two days later, my despondency diminished by ample rest and my determination somewhat weakened by the dictates of hunger and thirst, I decided that I could at least check out the place before leaving, and I timidly started exploring my surroundings. This brought me in contact with another resident, and the severity of my culture shock can be gauged by the fact that in realizing that he was a "fellow European" I felt such a sense of joy, relief, and gratitude that I practically never again left his side, and three months later we were married.

In retrospect, I think that my culture shock was actually amplified by this experience, since it compelled me to try to contemporaneously negotiate two cultural realities that were both quite alien to me: the Japanese one of day-to-day living and the English one my husband represented. At the same time, though, having a partner providing continuous emotional support gave both of us the opportunity to dispassionately analyze our reactions to the Japanese milieu, while the discovery of cultural differences between us increased our sensitivity to nuances of behavior and schooled us in the tolerance for diversity and sense of humor that alone can successfully lead to overcoming culture shock.

In my case, though, the reactions I found myself experiencing in Japan touched off an intellectual chain reaction. My culture shock filled me at first with surprise and then with indignation. How could a Japan "expert," as I still considered myself, find herself so totally lost in a culture lovingly studied for years? How could my knowledge of Japanese language, history, literature, and philosophy be of no use in helping me adjust to a setting I thought I was quite familiar with? How could I react so negatively toward a society I considered a sort of spiritual "second home"? But, above all, how was I ever to find a way to sort out the blooming, buzzing confusion that seemed to surround me and try to get on with the research required by my project?

The answers to these questions did not come quickly or easily, but I increasingly found help through a disciplinary approach I had known only vaguely before arriving in Japan, the approach of cultural anthropology. By becoming familiar with some of this discipline's concepts, not only did I start to understand and resolve my culture shock but I also began formulating strategies through which I could successfully negotiate the reality of Japanese culture. As I began to recognize the cultural matrix of particular patterns of behavior, I came to see their connectedness and to accept their "necessity," and all the frustration and irritation I had experienced in dealing with them became diluted in the sheer pleasure of solving an intellectual puzzle. As time went by, I actually found myself looking for circumstances that would test my understanding. As I gradually trained myself in the fundamental anthropological skills of "attending, observing, registering, and correlating," I discovered that I could now look on cultural misunderstanding as a pleasurable challenge rather than a source of stress.

Predictably, the area in which I had experienced the greatest difficulties—much more serious than the discomfort initially created by the noise and the crowds—had to do with role expectations, particularly in relation to my scholarly activities. I had arrived in Japan as a young professional, with specific projects to accomplish. I expected to fit easily into an academic community where mutual intellectual stimulation would be freely exchanged, on a collegial basis. Instead, I soon found that my comparatively young age and the circumstances of my residence in Japan had automatically labeled me as an "apprentice." As such I had been assigned to a number of senior scholars whose role was not only to aid my learning but also "to look after me" in every sense of the word. Furthermore, their instruction would not be imparted through the scintillating intellectual exchanges I had so often engaged in with my Italian professors but through what first looked to be endless, aimless sessions of small talk, typically shared with a group of other "disciples," who seemed chiefly interested in providing a passive audience and were not even trying to discuss their knowledge, opinions, or ideas.

Although I felt it my duty to fulfill my hosts' expectations and I tried to play the "disciple" role to the best of my ability, for almost two years I found this experience utterly bewildering. It was only when my anthropological investigations led me to see the connection between socialization practices, sense of self, and definition of social role that I began to see how the Japanese teaching/learning style—through personal contact in the context of a hierarchical, paternalistic relationship—fitted so well with other aspects of Japanese society. In fact, I then became convinced that in Japan the teacher-student relationship encapsulates so many facets of the overall cultural "script" that it is perceived as a general model for interpersonal relations. Consequently, I believed its study would provide critical insight into the fundamental characteristics of Japanese culture, and I started to study it in earnest by becoming an "apprentice" to a number of "masters." In this area of behavior, as in several others that had created profound puzzlement, anthropology had led me from frustration to understanding, and I felt privileged to have found such a useful "key."

I really believe that the way I discovered anthropology gave an unusual twist to an experience that could have been lived very differently. Not having been formally trained in this discipline, I was able to explore it in an idiosyncratic way, picking and choosing concepts and approaches totally on my own and having the opportunity of immediately testing them in a "total immersion" situation. Being in Japan not as an anthropologist doing field research but as an Orientalist pursuing a literary project, I never developed the type of ambiguous rapport with "the natives" that cultural investigations often engender. My desire to understand Japanese society was not a requirement of research but a prerequisite for mental equilibrium. Thus I never resented the enormous investment of time and effort it required, and I never tired of doing it. Above all, I never perceived any aspect of Japanese culture as a "problem" to be studied; rather, I clearly recognized *myself* as the problem, insofar as I needed to learn to fit into Japanese society to be able to pursue my scholarly project. I did a lot of participant observation in Japan, but it hardly was the application of a particular disciplinary technique;

I was as a child growing up, badly wanting to participate in the culture in which I found myself. Observation and relentless analysis were simply the only ways to earn an admission ticket.

As a consequence of all this, I never looked at cultural anthropology merely as an academic subject or as a field of professional specialization. Rather, I came to consider it a sort of "intellectual life preserver," an eminently applied science through which I could understand my husband, get on with my studies, and learn to live comfortably in a foreign country. At the same time, I also think that the fact that I "discovered" anthropology in Japan colored my disciplinary orientation. First, it strongly biased me toward a "cultural" rather than "social" approach, and second, it called my attention to the overall homogeneity and integration of cultural patterns, particularly as expressed in nonverbal and paraverbal behavior. Because I had to figure out the organization of Japanese culture "from the inside," through description and interpretation of details rather than through the abstract comparison of general characteristics, I found the model of culture originally developed by Boas, and still at the basis of the American anthropological tradition, much more useful than any other. Furthermore, this model proved especially effective because Japanese culture lends itself particularly well to an inductive, behaviorally focused analysis.

Japan is a very homogeneous society in which strict conformity to standardized rules of behavior is highly valued and commonly practiced. Partly because of this, the Japanese are experts at carrying on "silent dialogues" through the sophisticated modulation of nonverbal behavior, and they are extremely skillful at extracting symbolic meaning from the most varied aspects of experience. Japanese behavior is simultaneously so ritualized and rich in symbolic nuances that an outsider observer can not escape an overpowering feeling of being in the midst of a high-level balletic performance, where everyone knows exactly how to contribute to the overall effect. As a result, in becoming increasingly familiar with Japanese culture, one comes to associate it with the image of a *tableau vivant,* a pattern of patterns, the best possible illustration for Ruth Benedict's concept of "cultural configuration." Furthermore, in dealing with the Japanese, someone with a growing interest in anthropology as a discipline—like me at the time—is strengthened in the belief that a culture can truly be studied and understood simply by observing and analyzing the behavior of its members.

ENCOUNTERING ETHNICITY

While the insights of cultural anthropology helped me considerably in adjusting to Japan, just as the experience of Japanese culture molded my basic anthropological perspective, what finally convinced me to pursue this discipline professionally—and to do so in the United States—was a trip to Hawaii. I went there from the East, since at the expiration of my scholarship I had decided to stay on in Japan to teach and do research. I stayed on for more than seven years, and the trip to Hawaii was just a holiday, but again, a chance experience gave a powerful spin to the trajectory of my life and of my intellectual growth. What I found in Hawaii was the phenomenon of ethnic variation. Obviously I was already aware of the reality of ethnicity, but it was only by seeing it correlated to minority status in the context of a truly multiethnic society that I perceived its great relevance to the understanding of culture.

Arriving in Hawaii from Japan made me look at the Japanese-Americans I came to know there with particular interest. Clearly they were neither Japanese nor American but something new and unique. What particularly struck me, though, was that what made them unique was not the superimposition of new patterns of behavior on the Japanese but rather the subtle way their Japaneseness had been—in my eyes at least—both subtly transformed and reinforced.

This conclusion was reached, I believe, because being attuned to Japanese nonverbal behavior I could see it reproduced faithfully, albeit in a simplified form, in the behavior of the Japanese-Americans I met in Hawaii. What *had* changed, in some cases quite dramatically, was verbal behavior, especially as a vehicle for the expression of values and beliefs. However, it seemed to me that a recognizable Japanese behavioral style was very much present and that among in-group members the decoding of its underlying symbolic meaning proceeded undisturbed by possible superimposed verbal disclaimers, as if it were operating below awareness and ahead of any conscious labeling process. I would see, for example, Japanese-American women forcefully argue for female equality and independence just as they nonverbally gave out messages of docility, other-directedness, and submission to male authority— messages that seemed to set the "tone" of interaction with other Japanese-Americans much more strongly than their verbal counterpart.

The observations I gathered during my visit to Hawaii considerably strengthened my inclination toward looking at culture as a system of communication and also gave me some basic ideas on how to define ethnicity in relation to culture. In particular, I remember becoming very excited about thinking that if indeed the original patterns of nonverbal and paraverbal behavior are maintained across generations of people born and raised in a culture different from their ancestral one, then they may constitute the very core of cultural behavioral style and thus be the key to understanding the dynamics of cultural membership and identity.

Subsequent research experiences in various parts of Asia, England, and Italy confirmed my original feeling that no matter what level of assimilation an ethnic group achieves, group identity is essentially maintained through the perpetuation of a set of microbehavioral patterns that are learned during the very early years of life. Although largely unrecognized as bonding factors, these patterns seem to determine both self-identification and group cohesion by generating a recognizable behavioral style that can be called on to establish group boundaries when necessary for ideological reasons. I also concluded that if we could trace the trajectory by which behavioral style changes during the process of acculturation, we would reach a better understanding of how it comes into being in the first place. As time went by, I increasingly felt that to test many of these ideas I needed to do firsthand research among ethnic groups living in a typically multiethnic society; that is when I decided to come to the United States.

Ethnic diversity is not, of course, a peculiarly American phenomenon, but the type of ethnic groups one finds in America and the ideological definition of ethnicity that has been developing within the context of American society warrant special attention. Most of the latent, emerging, or established ethnic groups I had occasion to study in Asia and Europe have not experienced relocation. They live in areas ancestrally theirs, and the characteristics of the land they inhabit are very much a part of their sense of uniqueness. Often, as the advocates of separatism among them argue, they are simply "nations without states," groups that have become part of larger national systems to which they do not feel they really belong. The situation I found in the United States is very different. With the exception of the Native Americans and of the Mexicans originally living in what has now become the American Southwest, all of the ethnic groups one finds in the United States are the result of migration. Furthermore, as a consequence of the civil rights movement and the nationwide social unrest of the 1960s and early 1970s, there has emerged in the United States a "minority group" ideology. According to this, the political elite has recognized the cultural diversity of a few ethnic groups, has regulated their existence through the creation of well-defined boundaries around them—first and foremost by declaring them "official minorities"—and has institutionalized the presumptive process of their assimilation through a program of majority-selected incentives for socioeconomic advancement. As a result, ethnicity and minority status—with all the socially uncomplimentary connotations of these terms—have become equated in the minds of many Americans, just as the latent consciousness of ethnic heterogeneity leads many to believe that there is no such thing as an "American culture." These contradictions seem to *demand* anthropological analysis, and from my first days in America I believed that any kind of research conducted here would prove particularly rewarding. Furthermore, having decided to formalize my interest in anthropology by entering a graduate program at UCLA, I found that my excitement about doing research in the country in which Franz Boas had developed the anthropological approach I considered so attractive was compounded by that of studying in an academic setting that had actually produced a number of distinguished Boasian anthropologists. Because of all this, I saw coming to America not only as an opportunity for exciting research but also as both the fulfillment of a fantasy and the repayment of an intellectual debt. I did not know, though, that this experience would lead me to insights that entirely redimensioned my views of culture and of anthropological research.

CUTURAL PARTICIPATION AND ANALYSIS

After leaving Japan and before coming to the United States, I had gone back to Italy for a while, and I had lived for a period in my husband's home country, England. Also, over the ten years preceding my journey to America, I had visited a score of Asian and European countries. With this experience to back me up and with the knowledge provided by years of anthropological study and research, including professional involvement in intercultural training, I fully expected to be "vaccinated" against culture shock, but I learned soon enough that this is one reaction not assuaged by training. Besides, if now I at least had the consolation of being familiar with the symptoms of culture shock, this time they were combined with a psychological crisis for which I was not at all prepared.

My decision to study anthropology in the United States had not been anchored to any amount of practical knowledge of the American educational system or even of the current characteristics of American intellectual life. With the ethnocentrism typical of someone making an emotional choice, I had expected that my study experience in America would closely resemble those I had already undergone in Italy and Japan, with all their characteristics of elitism and exclusiveness I took so much for granted. I most definitely was not prepared for the atmosphere of an American public university campus, set by what seemed to me an incredibly large number of incredibly young undergraduates. I was not prepared for the frank and democratic American acceptance of the characteristics of mass education, including what I considered an enormous amount of bureaucratic complexity. I was not prepared to find that educational quality could be so openly and directly linked to its financial cost. I was not prepared to see such a large portion of both the undergraduate and graduate student population consist of foreigners. I was not prepared for the businesslike, impersonal way students were treated by campus staff and even by many professors. Most especially, I was not prepared for being considered "just another foreign graduate student" and to have to deal on a daily basis with people who were unknowingly belittling my background and experience—including years of fieldwork and university teaching—and whose behavior I so often found either patronizing or dismissive.

With hindsight I now think that this was an extremely useful experience, but its value was paid in frustration, humiliation, and exasperation. Again, I was lucky in being able to share it with my husband—who had also entered a graduate program—and in having the help and support of an outstanding group of academic mentors. The chair of my sponsoring committee, the late Professor Hiroshi Wagatsuma, was particularly instrumental in helping me maintain a measure of mental health. He himself, Japanese-born and trained at the most elite Japanese institution, Tokyo University, had undergone experiences similar to mine when first entering the United States, and after many years of teaching and living here, he was still vividly aware of the difficulties created by cultural dissonance.

Talking with Professor Wagatsuma was excellent therapy, but more important, in listening to the anecdotes with which he could so brilliantly exemplify his analyses of American culture, I started to realize that my problems were essentially *cultural* and that this experience, albeit painful, was also providing me with a great chance for reaching new insights about the craft of anthropology itself. After I had suffered greatly from what I considered attacks to my sense of personal worth, I finally realized that this was happening only because I had not framed this experience in anthropological terms. Why was I taking "native" definitions—of friendship, scholarly work, or success—so very seriously? Had I not learned the lesson of relativism and of the inevitability of ethnocentrism? Where was my use of the fundamental anthropological skill of balancing the emic and etic points of view? Why was I getting irritated by the Americans making fun of my accent when I had taken perfectly in my stride the Japanese incessantly pointing and laughing at my Roman nose or at my overall foreignness? These were all questions I found myself "stonewalling," until I realized that I was embarrassed by their simple answers. The fact was that, because American culture was typically Western, I had related to it as if it were my own and was then cut to the core by its "betrayal."

The whole problem emerged from the question of participation: Since I had come to America as a student, I wanted to fully participate in the culture in this role, but according to *my own* culture-specific definition of it. Thus, I had encountered great problems in areas of behavior particularly related to the definition of that role. The quantification drive underlying the educational system baffled me; the profound anti-intellectualism of even the most dedicated American student bewildered me; and the prevalence of anecdote over analysis, of simplicity over complexity, of concreteness over abstraction, and of detail over depth in the teaching and studying of social science vexed me. Here I was, in one of the best anthropology programs in the country, and all my peers would talk about whenever we met socially were other people, sports, money, or sex. If professional matters were ever discussed, they would concern grades, number of publications, or job prospects. If one became involved in a research project, people seemed interested in knowing only who funded and administered it. If one took a new course, people would want to know what the instructor was like.

While my initial adjustment problems in Japanese academia had to do with acceptance of my role as the feudal retainer for munificent intellectual lords, now I felt plunged back into the nervous, immature atmosphere of my junior high school days. But whereas in Japan I had managed to detach my sense of self from the behavior that was required from me, and I had in fact taken pride in becoming an "impeccably cultural performer," now I could not seem to do the same. This realization led me to a long process of cultural self-analysis, at the end of which I came to better understand not only the salient characteristics of my cultural background but also all the hidden epistemological agendas that had colored my research until then. In turn, this made me look at the ethnographic enterprise from a new point of view, and I came to see in sharp relief some of its more common limitations: the concentration on the study of exotic, marginal, or socially deviant groups, clearly different from the ones we, the researchers, belong to; our common practice of "the field trip," always implying a physical demarcation between "our" territory and that of the people to be studied; and the use we make of our study of cultural specificity to acquire prestige within academic worlds that are themselves culture-specific. Indeed, a certain kind of anthropological research started to seem to me at this point a rigged intellectual game with limited possible returns. On the other hand, I also came to appreciate that once the test of *real* participant observation is successfully negotiated, anthropological analysis can provide the deepest understanding of the human experience.

Now I fully realized for the first time that culture is not a sort of house we can enter and leave at will. Culture defines the parameters of all human expressions, and, like a chronic disease, we always carry it with us. Thus, there are no extracultural standpoints from which to do cultural analysis. My understanding of Japanese culture had been filtered through the lenses of my Italian background, and the whole process was being repeated in America. However, both in Japan and in the United States I had not had the wish and the opportunity to distance myself emotionally from the setting of my cultural analysis. In Japan, for a variety of reasons—including the extreme physical "foreignness" of the setting—I had managed to become a real participant and to maintain an ethnographic detachment. But in America I had fallen into the trap of fully validating native categories and then resenting them.

Understanding the dynamics of this process helped me resolve most of my day-to-day frustrations and made me realize that anthropological practice, per se, does not necessarily lead to overcoming ethnocentrism. In fact, by "institutionalizing" the distance between the researcher and the people being studied, anthropological practice may subtly reinforce ethnocentrism. But, if anthropological practice is supplemented by the test of real participant observation, one can begin to comprehend the enormous scope of cultural constraints. At this point the anthropologist truly becomes an impeccable "professional stranger." From this point, however, one neither can "turn off" the anthropological lenses through which all experiences become framed nor "go home again," simply because the very concept of "home," as a privileged native culture, has been totally deconstructed through ethnographic detachment.

EXPLORING AMERICAN CULTURE

Figuring all this out took the best part of my first four years of residence in the United States, including a lengthy trip to Italy at the end of the third year. By the end of this period I had completed my coursework and taken my doctoral qualifying exams, and I was doing exciting research on several fronts.

As I mentioned previously, my original project had to do with trying to trace the trajectory of change affecting the communication patterns of ethnic group members living in a multiethnic society. Because of my previous experience, I had initially planned to study the acculturation of the Japanese-Americans. However, the very hypothesis at the basis of my research—that ethnicity is perpetuated through the maintenance of microbehavioral patterns acquired so early in life that they become almost unconscious—led me to consider the necessity of selecting for my analysis an ethnic group *not* labeled as a minority, to demonstrate that retention of an idiosyncratic ethnic style has nothing to do with social labeling or group militancy. Also, particularly under the influence of Professor Wagatsuma, I had become increasingly interested in the issue of "native anthropology," and I was intrigued by the way it related to the study of ethnicity. Specifically, being Italian myself, I started wondering what it would be like to study the Italian-Americans. Would my perceptions of this group be different from those of Italian-American scholars, and if so, how? And how would my observations compare with those gathered by researchers of totally different ethnic backgrounds, such as, for example, members of the Anglo majority?

While I was still trying to decide the focus of my research, I was lucky enough to become involved with a project investigating the health-maintenance practices of various American groups of Asian ancestry. I was able to use my "Asian expertise" within that context, and I decided to concentrate on the Italian-Americans for my doctoral dissertation research. For the next several years, these were the two areas of investigation in which I was formally engaged. At the same time, however, the exploration of American culture as a whole remained my informal, but no less exciting or demanding, objective. I soon learned that revealing this objective to American fellow anthropologists-in-training was not a good idea. In particular, my asking for their professional insights into their own culture seemed to create great embarrassment. In line with this, the unwritten rule about anthropology graduate work in most of the academic institutions I came to know during this period was that "real" anthropological research is done abroad. On the other hand, foreign students—especially from "exotic" Asian and African countries—would be encouraged to study aspects of their own cultures. Furthermore, I noticed that even discussing the topic of my formal research on ethnicity would create quite a bit of uneasiness; Americans, including American anthropologists, simply did not seem to expect that a foreigner may be here to study their culture, and ethnicity was certainly one of the aspects of the culture they least wished to discuss.

As for my Italian-American research subjects, while fully informed of the aim of my project and of the observation techniques I would employ, they were quick to let me know how they thought ethnicity should be studied. Although they always put up very graciously with my observation sessions, they also ended up "convincing" me that I should really interview them about their values and beliefs. In effect, all through my explorations of American culture, I repeatedly found a common popular concern with the ideational realm, an attitude almost opposite to the Japanese preoccupation with behavioral norms. A great many Americans seem to believe that "ideas make the person" and because ideas can and do change, people can continuously reinvent themselves. Perhaps because of this belief, the idea of American culture as a stable configuration is not commonly accepted, and even members of minority groups feel that their identity is a matter of "negotiation."

On my part, however, I found that applying a complex set of micro-behavioral observation techniques, I not only could document the remarkable retention of an ethnic-specific behavioral style across generations of Italian-Americans but I was also able to find relevant commonalities in the behavior of people observed in random social settings, from a doctor's visiting room to a barbecue party and from a department store to a university campus, thus gathering evidence of a system of recognizably American behavioral patterns. Also, the academic program I had joined gathered a large number of advanced foreign students, and it was very instructive and therapeutic to exchange notes with them on American culture in general and on the subculture of American academia in particular.

I especially enjoyed monitoring the reactions of Asian students, since I was often able to predict them, and I sometimes came to share these reactions. One of these had to do with American humor; neither I nor my Asian fellow students—especially the Japanese among them—could get used to the constant barrage of sarcastic put-downs Americans seem cheerfully to accept as "joking." After being caught in a particularly virulent exchange of wisecracks, one of these friends once told me he privately referred to it as "jockeying," as in jockeying for power and control, and I still think this is an accurate definition of what goes on behind the smiles. I recognized a distinct continuity between American humor and its Anglo-Irish counterpart. I had experienced problems with a certain brand of British joking all through the time I had lived in England. But what I found most surprising in the American penchant for sarcasm is its use by people who seem typically characterized by great personal vulnerability and a very shaky sense of self-worth, so that humorous repartee becomes a sort of voluntary "social flagellation."

Actually, I have often wondered whether Americans do harbor a streak of Puritan masochism; "No pain no gain" sounds profoundly suspect to my Mediterranean ears. Certainly the dictates of extreme individualism, combined with ideological rigidity *and* social heterogeneity, seem to lead almost inevitably to a "culture in pain." During my years in graduate school, I observed many casualties of the enormous pressure people live under. After maintaining a decent GPA while putting up with all the wisecracking, the showing off, the self-promotion, the undercutting of potential competitors, and the sexual and ethnic tensions, some students would just suddenly "disappear." "Oh, he moved to the Coast. . . . She has found a good job. . . . He ran out of money. . . . She just dropped out" people would say, and in a few days, the person would apparently be totally forgotten. When confronted about this cavalier attitude toward evident casualties of a ruthlessly competitive system, people would reply "You gotta learn not to care too much. People move, start new lives, don't keep up. If you care you get hurt." To me it all sounded like the rationalizations of people hardened by life in a war zone.

Foreigners often comment favorably on the "energy" one senses in this country. It is certainly real, but its flip side is tension. When I first came here, one of the things that particularly struck me was that strangers who accidentally make eye contact—in the street, in shops, on public transportation—will speak or at least smile to each other, something unthinkable in either Europe or Japan. Americans say it is just a way to be friendly, but to me this always seems a touching effort at establishing an amicable truce with potential enemies, as if to avoid a likely confrontation. Similarly, I now find it rather odd or strange that American public speakers almost inevitably begin their presentations with a little joke, but from a European point of view, this is a strategy that seems to betray both performance anxiety and a clumsy attempt at courting favor. It is certainly a very different opening gambit from the British one, which requires a strong statement of fact, or the Italian one, which can be either an idiosyncratic statement of opinion or an outright complaint.

Once I started to teach, the level of performance anxiety American students live with really became evident. To comfort my classes, I often tell them that in Italy examination results are always publicly posted, that most university exams involve a personal interview—at which the professor frankly expresses her or his overall opinion of you, whether positive or negative—and that most of these interview sessions are large public events, so that there may be a lot of witnesses to your downfall. They listen in disbelief and groan in real pain. Certainly, the characteristics of American society that critics traditionally bemoan—the personal isolation, the psychological insecurity, the ruthless competition, the liability of social status, and the intolerance for diversity—justify this anxiety. But, in my view, there are two factors that uniquely handicap the pursuit of a contented life in this culture: One is the commitment to ideological integrity over interpersonal harmony, and the other is the lack of cultural self-awareness. Obviously these perceptions are strongly influenced by my comparative framework, in turn created by my Italian background and Japanese experience. However, the "natives" themselves are ready to admit that ideas, values, and beliefs are taken very seriously in this country, and, in so doing, the human factor is repressed or trampled over and much personal unhappiness results. Shortly before arriving here, I briefly visited the Soviet Union, and I cannot shake the impression that American and Soviet cultures are unexpectedly similar in this respect. At a deep level not influenced by political changes, they share a penchant for "radical utilitarianism," a tendency toward measuring everything in relation to ideological goals, disregarding human and aesthetic values in the process.

What seems to me uniquely American, however, is a profound disbelief in systemic social constraints and, in particular, in the reality of an indigenous culture. For years I have been systematically polling students, acquaintances, and miscellaneous informants on their perceptions of American culture, and I must conclude that denying that an American culture exists seems to be one of the most consistent local cultural traits. But Americans are very interested in themselves, and if a foreigner asks about seemingly peculiar cultural characteristics—Why do people eat popcorn at the movies? Why do coffee cups often get refilled free in restaurants? Why do people always get invited to social events in couples? Why is ethnicity only recognized in minority groups? Why is youth considered better than maturity?—they take pause and seem willing to start looking at their behavior from a new perspective. That is when teaching anthropology becomes truly exciting. By openly discussing my perceptions of American culture and by encouraging students to analyze how these perceptions may be related to my cultural background, I can lead them to turn their ethnographic lenses to various aspects of their own daily experience.

The point of all this is that I have come to believe that the anthropological perspective is a "way of life," as well as the outlook of a specific discipline. Being an anthropologist can simply mean getting a certain type of diploma and performing certain prescribed activities according to the expectations agreed on by a certain professional community. But it can also mean trying to understand the very matrices of our behavior and being able, if not to escape the mazeways our native culture has trained us to walk, at least to analyze the entire process, dissect its formulation, and contemplate its results. Anthropological knowledge can certainly increase mutual tolerance but only if we are prepared to train the field glasses on our own cultural peculiarities and define them as such. To achieve this, it helps to undergo the test of *real* participant observation, but I believe that with the right guidance, aspiring anthropologists can be trained to reap the rewards of "continuous ethnographic alert" without having to suffer the pain of prolonged cultural dissonance.

There is, however, one potentially disturbing fact that must be taken into serious consideration when embarking on the ethnographic enterprise. That is the realization that if culture determines the framework of all our expressions, it must also affect our cognitive processes. This implies that any intellectual endeavor, including anthropological theorizing (or writing about anthropological experiences, as in this article), is culturally colored. Fortunately, human beings have an adaptive capacity for thinking they understand each other even when they are instead steadily mistranslating incoming messages. But this does not have to be the only way to keep intercultural interaction open. I am quite convinced that if anthropological research methods can be clarified and systematically applied, if we develop careful guidelines for the cultural self-analysis of aspiring anthropologists, if we relentlessly explore the process by which behavioral style emerges, and if we find a way to elucidate the boundaries between culture and ethnicity, our discipline can live up to the promise its founders felt assured it had.

I also believe it is particularly important to analyze cultural settings not usually considered "for anthropological consumption." Ethnographic reports on French or American culture have a very different impact on the Western reader than, say, descriptions of the Ik or Yanomamo cultures. Whether we want to admit it or not, the latter tend to become, at best, abstract metaphors for the human condition. The pervasive reality of culture can only be truly appreciated when you call people's attention to its *local* expressions, and if this can be done by native and nonnative researchers in a position of real participation, so much the better. Bronislaw Malinowski once said that anthropology is the discipline of the sense of humor. This is a particularly nice definition, I think, if we complement it with the lesson of real participant observation. If we can identify our own cultural foibles and still smile at ourselves, we can also learn to live with the strangeness of assorted "cultural others," since we will be able to see the culture as just a reflection of our own. This is the perspective I gained from my exploration of American culture, and how much value I give to it is self-evident: I am still here.

America for Americans

RIK PINXTEN
University of Ghent, Belgium

In his thought-provoking critique, Professor Pinxten begins with a commentary on American systems of politeness and rudeness, leading into the academic system as a model of the corporate world. He also poignantly discusses the differences between European and American ethnographic methodologies and the decline or sublimation of American intellectualism, which is well supported by the examples provided during the recent Persian Gulf crisis.

Rik Pinxten *is a professor of Anthropology at the University of Ghent, Belgium. He was raised and studied in Belgium but spent nearly two years in the United States, mainly on the Navajo Reservation in Arizona. Professor Pinxten received two Ph.D.s in Philosophy and Anthropology from the University of Ghent (1975, 1980).*

In the fall of 1976, I flew into New York for the first time. The immigration services at the airport were absolutely awful. After a long wait with other sleepy, stinking passengers from all over the world, my girlfriend and I finally reached the counter and our first encounter with a representative of the American government. My girlfriend had a tourist visa, and mine was for an exchange fellow. We were planning to stay for a year, and we told the officer of our intention. Immediately the man flew into a rage, scolding my girlfriend for trying to sneak into the country. He threatened to put her back on the plane if she intended to enter the country for more than six months. The man probably had a problem at home, or he assumed, quite ethnocentrically, that everybody who comes here tries to immigrate into the United States. The experience was horrible. We stood there pleading for twenty minutes, despairing that we would miss our connection to Chicago, even if we were able to pass the bully posing as a civil servant. Gradually, the films we had seen about Ellis Island appeared in a different light. Silently, we felt sorry for those who had to go through the ordeal over the years, and we hated our immigration officer for the misery and hardship he seemed to have caused generations of immigrants who came before us. There and then we decided that if we would ever think of migrating to the United States permanently, this officer would have to convince us of the fact that Americans have a heart.

On that occasion we finally got through customs, and we made our plane to Chicago just in time. At O'Hare we were met by an American colleague, who later became a good friend. His darling wife was with him. They picked us up and drove for an endless last portion of our trip to their home, where we had the privilege to stay for a few days. When we arrived at their home, the first thing the wife asked was, "Do you want to take a shower?" We decided that the culture shock we were to have with Native Americans could not be more intense that what we had experienced that very first day.

"CAN I HELP YOU, HONEY?"

Belgians are rather formal toward each other. In public life you don't address somebody you don't know in a jovial way. As a general rule, you don't greet strangers in the street, except for businesslike matters. Because of this background in "stiff" Europe, the superficial friendliness in shops and in public services in the United States came as a complete surprise.

People working in the post office are notoriously unfriendly in most European countries. The myth goes around that this is part of their very self-image, so that any post office worker who respects himself tries to be more unfriendly than his colleagues. The competition is tough, and it is often difficult to determine which postal worker is best at it. Hence, it is a shattering experience to go into an American post office and be addressed in a friendly, social way. It actually feels nice, and, at first, I had the urge to strike up a deep conversation with the unique civil servant who was nevertheless friendly to the customers.

That same day, my girlfriend came home from a shopping tour and described one of her exotic adventures. When visiting an ordinary supermarket, she was "approached" by a stranger, who addressed these intimate words to her, "Can I help you with something, honey?" Obviously, her first impression was that this young man had unspeakable plans for her and found no better opportunity to express them than in a supermarket.

After a day or two, we knew that this was the rule in this country and not the exception. People seem to think of each other as equals with regard to business relationships, social services, and the like. Neither the customer nor the service provider feels punished by the interaction. This still strikes me as a decent view on interpersonal relationships. At the same time, and rather obviously, it is a superficial friendliness. It took me some time to figure out what it is, how deep or shallow it is, and why it still gives you a good feeling. I now think it ties into the atmosphere of obligatory optimism that is so striking in this young country.

A similar expression of this open mentality can be discerned in the attitude toward academics. (Because I had contacts mainly with academics and with Native Americans, I feel I cannot speak for most other segments of American society.) A striking characteristic of American academia is that young scholars are given a chance. It seems to be a rule within the community of scholars that fresh brains are needed at any time. The space can sometimes be filled with candidates from one's own flock, but foreigners are allowed at least as much. This is, odd as it may seem for the American public, rare in Europe. In my experience, the relative openness for new thoughts and approaches is striking. A correlate of this attitude is that older scholars will indicate where you can get funds, who is the most interesting person for you to meet on campus, and so on. European academia is more factionalized to the point that contacts with a colleague are often terminated if you are affiliated with the "enemy" camp. I am not sure which attitude is better in the long run, but the experience of difference is intense.

As I said at the beginning of this appraisal, the openness seems to be restricted to fresh or new members of the scholarly society. A tinge of exoticism may be spotted here. Any professor is proud and indeed gains esteem by showing off to his colleagues the unpredictable and innovative candidate who landed on his table. I understood that it gives you prestige to have visitors from abroad and to be able to exhibit them in the university community. The ideas that they bring are welcomed with the curiosity that is directed at any novelty in this land of pioneers. Coming from Europe seems to add to the prestige of the candidate, since that still is the continent where, in the minds of many American academics, most ideas are born. So the door is opened a little bit for us outsiders to perform our number. If someone then wants to hang on and compete for a job, he or she must enter the so-called "rat race." As I was reminded by several Europeans who took that step, the friendliness and openness suddenly disappear at that point, since one then becomes a competitor and ceases to be a curiosity.

When I compare with my impressions of the European system on these points, I am inclined to make the following balance: The American academic system has a marginal space for novelty, whereas the European system is closed to a very high degree. At the same time, American scholars are not really interested in the intellectual input of novices, but they want (or need?) to give them a forum and, hence, at least offer a chance. The European scholar is interested in at least his or her own contribution to the great tradition of knowledge (preferably rewriting it in the scope of his or her own pedigree) and allows the novice within these confines only. For example, one can write a book review in *Man* stating that such and such is really not worth reading because it is clearly not Oxford vintage anthropology and get away with it in the United Kingdom. Anybody who would do that in the *American Anthropologist* would be ridiculed by the rest of the American anthropological community. On the one hand, this lack of factionalism allows for new ideas and provides openings for unknown scholars. On the other hand, it seems to go hand in hand with a lesser degree of engagement or a lesser attachment to "a cause" in the U.S. system. To decide which one allows for a better climate to work in is an altogether different problem, which I cannot begin to solve here.

SERIOUSLY: WHAT ARE THE FACTS?

I have to grant that the telephone was invented and implemented by an American. In contrast, there is no certainty as to who invented letter writing. For all I know, it may have been a European. In my career as a scholar in Europe, I must have written over five thousand letters to various colleagues around the world (in some twenty years not counting administrative notes, which we all equally resent). It is indeed common among Europeans to correspond in writing about themes of research, ideas, first drafts, and so on. My American colleagues, however, rarely respond in writing. Americans prefer the telephone. I am convinced that there is no deep resentment or contempt on the part of the European against this technological wonder but rather a different view on the nature of the messages that are best conveyed by it. My ethnographic data on this point indicate that Americans use the telephone both for emotional and intellectual contact with people and for businesslike messages. It is not rare to hear somebody explain a theory or brief the addressee about important progress in a research endeavor. Phoning seems to be a superior (easier? quicker?) way to transfer information and to further the thought process, second only to actually meeting people. I once encountered an anthropologist who believed ethnography could be better because he found a shack with a phone connection at his field site. I can understand how one feels safer with the knowledge that one can reach the "outside world" at any time, but how can the quality of research be enhanced by this facility? If anything, it may detract from engaging fully in the field experience (but maybe that is an old-fashioned European romanticism).

Furthermore, the very use of computer technology for writing and reliance on the telephone gave me a hint at the difference in intellectual culture here and there. The use of the computer in or close to the field is an illustration of the same feature of American intellectual tradition. Both the growing prominence of the personal computer (PC) in the field and the dependence on telephone accessibility imply a specific (and most often hidden or unconscious) view of knowledge. Indeed, it has been my experience that American anthropologists are and remain, first and foremost, empiricists. There is a deep belief in the possibility of learning about the world (including the world of "the Other") by getting the facts first. And the facts are "out there to be discovered." The telephone is the adequate instrument to transfer the kind of knowledge believed to be purely "factual." The computer, as a large, fast notebook, is then, in the eyes of my American colleagues, a sort of private telephone with a large memory. The two devices fit the epistemology of the American ethnographer. They do not, at least not at a prominent level, have the same value for European researchers.

An illustration from my own fieldwork with Native Americans will make clear what I mean by the differences in epistemology. As a European, I was slowly getting involved in vague and open-ended discussions about cosmology and philosophy with Navajos. Granted, this way of doing fieldwork is sometimes a hazard, and misunderstanding proved to be the rule rather than the exception, at least in the beginning. Prior to entering the field, an American colleague had tackled me regarding methodology: How was I going to reach my data? By means of what concrete empirical methodology? He was not really interested in the quest I was engaged in but turned immediately to the point of methodology. In order to gain respectability and validity in any research, the "how" seemed to be more important to him (and others) than the "what."

Notwithstanding his advice, I kept probing for a good formulation of my problem in the field rather than bothering myself with the details of method and technique. The funny thing was that in the first weeks of my fieldwork, several Native American consultants reacted in exactly the same way as my American colleague. At one point one of them said quite explicitly, "You ask the wrong questions. Anthropologists do it in such and such a way." His reference was to ethnographic techniques and standard question-and-answer procedures. This particular culture shock impressed my girlfriend and me so much that we accepted the rebuttal as a fact of the influence of "anthropological culture" on the natives. For the next few weeks, we only occasionally dared to bring up our "European" questions—that is, after "serious" work was done. The atmosphere changed radically after the death of one of the great old men we had the privilege of working with. Suddenly, the attitude of our Native American consultants changed. They were now more willing and sometimes even eager to talk to us about the "European" questions. One man even told us that, since we had worked on such important issues as the structure of the world with the old man, we now needed to have a more complete and varied picture. He was willing to provide it. In our appreciation, it proved to be the case that the "European" questions were relevant and even crucial to them, whether it was good "American" ethnography or not. Around the same time, we witnessed that some American researchers (young ones, to be honest) who had come out "to collect data on x or y" were severely fooled by the local residents they were interviewing and sometimes sent back home without further ado. What has all this to do with telephone and computers?

In my view, the phone and computer are the signs that allow me to find the cultural meaning of "being an intellectual in America." The fact that they are not exclusive at all to intellectuals is telling in and of itself, especially with regard to the status of this group in the United States. The American heirs to the intellectual tradition do not have their own privileged means and revered cult places. Indeed, they are common people, not very well-to-do; they are just middle-class people who have to fight for their right to survive while barely being tolerated by the money-makers. A friend once told me that "being a professor is a living but is rather looked down on by the better-situated people." He said, "If one cannot make it in business or in law or medicine in the United States, then the solution is to become a university professor." Hence, academics do not have high status, and they are believed to be satisfied with sharing some of the privileges the wealthy people can offer them. They do not treat books and writing with the (sometimes silly) reverence of Europeans and are satisfied to be allowed to use the more common media of the telephone and the computer. There is little respect for their engagement, and, in my opinion, most American intellectuals I met adapted to this status by showing a similar attitude to their own "trade."

Thus, the production of knowledge becomes a contingent and a more or less ordinary thing, not to be taken too seriously. It fits the nine-to-five schedule of most other jobs. Moreover, the terms and the subject matter of the trade are seen to be situated on approximately the same level as that of any other business. You will have to be quick, smart, and productive in this business in order to survive. You will have to "publish or perish," just as the businessperson has to sell or get out. Hence, the American academic wants to be a practical, businesslike, no-nonsense thinker who knows what he or she is talking about and who deals in clear, hard facts rather than in "wild speculations." In these terms, knowledge becomes, first and foremost, information (a drastic reduction in my view) and minitheories. At the same time, I see a high value being attached to applied research and to short-term research and a distrust in "merely" pure research, at least in the social sciences. Again, I think there is a healthy aspect to this particular academic subculture. It certainly helps to avoid romantic theories and sweeping ideologies posing as scientific interpretations. In this particular respect, Europeans can still benefit from the American critique. At the same time, I think it tremendously and unwarrantably reduces human intellectual scope. For one thing it produces tremendous boredom. Moreover, no grand theories, no vast inspirational schemes, and no possibly erroneous but thrilling and inspiring deep thoughts can flourish in such an intellectual soil. This may be why the mostly overvalued theories of French (and sometimes German) thinkers are time and again hailed in a rather uncritical way by American colleagues, who become "addicts" of structuralism and devotees of Sartre, Foucault, Heidegger, and other totalitarian thinkers of Europe. Recently, "systematic" postmodernists and Derrida followers have organized themselves in the United States, not being aware of the striking paradox of their own systematicity.

Of course, not all is better in "good old Europe." What I wanted to show is only that a particular intellectual climate, a specific subculture of academia, has grown in the United States, which changed the rules and practices of the *Aufklarung* (Enlightenment) to such an extent that one can now speak of the "scientific enterprise" in respectable circles. With this change, an important change in status and in research attitudes has taken hold. It remains to be seen what will become of the original values of "free research," the liberty of dissent, and the inexorable value of pure and theoretical research. So far and according to my opinion, these aspects are often "sacrificed" in favor of more "operational" standards. The elaborate and competitive grant system seems, if anything, to further this evolution.

I had the privilege to apply for a Wenner-Gren grant once, and I saw a series of grant proposals for other agencies (made by specialists in "proposal writing"). In all these cases, the same philosophy of concreteness was apparent. The idea or deep question does not matter most but rather the way the researcher is "actually going to do it." This emphasis excludes slightly crazy or unorthodox proposals, but the other side of the coin is that innovative ideas get precious little chance to be tried out. The pressure is toward conformity through recognizability.

THE INTELLECTUAL AS AN ALARM BELL

One of the greater aspects of the traditional intellectual, both in contemporary Russia (Solzhenitsyn) and in Europe (Bourdieu and Derrida but also Havel and many others), is that intellectuals still have a role in society at large as spokespersons or critics of their own culture. Philosophers and social scientists have occupied this role for the last two centuries and, within a new frame of science and philosophy, continue to do so. For one thing, the decolonization of the social sciences and the consciousness-raising of the social and cultural worker belong to the task of any respectable scientist on this side of the Atlantic Ocean. Without any doubt, the status of researcher has come under attack, but then it has been so for several centuries. In the United States, the older generations of writers and scientists have nourished such figures as Thoreau, Mead, and Bateson, but the recent attack on "liberalism" has left the few remaining heirs of this important tradition out in the cold. The lonely voice of Chomsky is heard primarily in Europe, while he is more or less banned from the United States. Bloom and others have declared that the "American intellectual" is dead, testifying to the fact that academic workers and subordinated specialists have taken his place. Especially at universities, the intellectuals are getting extremely rare. I can add some private experiences to make this view stand out more vividly.

In our long-term research with Navajo Indians, we came to know a lot of the white idealists who have devoted most of their lives to the benefit (at least they hope that will be the result) of Native Americans. Most of them started out with high values and great ideas. Many of them got frustrated over the years by the tremendous amount of "red tape" (a favorite term in these parts) they had to go through, but even more received a serious blow under the latest U.S. administrations. Programs were cancelled, funds were made dependent on success in accultura- tion and subordination, and a general attitude of efficiency in adapta- tion supplanted the broad and deeply felt liberalism that was there in the beginning. The Native Americans we saw over the years changed too. Some chose against their own tradition and hoped to be allowed in on the general affluence of white society.

However, since the late 1980s, a marked change in attitude has taken hold among the Navajo intellectuals and the whites who settled with them. Indeed, the more interesting intellectuals (at least from my point of view) are turning away from the value system of the American way of life and have become extremely selective with regard to the programs offered. Their attitudes are centered on reevaluating traditional standards and then carefully selecting from the facilities and technologies of white culture what will be useful and easily accommodate to their traditions. Put differently, they have stopped believing that there is a place for Native Americans in white American society, while realizing the inherent ad- vantages of their own way of life with the careful and selective incor- poration of elements from white culture. Hence, they adopt particular devices and technologies that are then used in an elaborate and explicit bicultural and bilingual educational scope. For the first time, Navajo adults are relearning their own language and have enrolled their children in bilingual schools. There has also been the introduction of technology for agriculture on a (hopefully) self-sufficient, cooperative plantation.

What I see in this process is a shift away from the old "melting- pot" idea toward a clear and conscious choice for self-supporting ex- istence next to the dominant white culture. With it goes a firm disbelief in the good intentions and in the respectability of the American democratic model. This, at least, is my appreciation, as an outsider. Moreover, it may not be specific to the United States. Some tendencies toward autonomy within a dominant culture can be discerned among the minorities in Europe, too, but the striking refusal to abide with white rule is most apparent. In a general way, the anthropologist in the field is implicated in this shift. The Navajo are more on their own and more proud than before, it would seem, and the anthropologist is less tolerated and more critically assessed as a foreigner. From the point of view of the

Navajo, this may be a major step forward. The anthropologists, at least in my experience, are becoming the odd ones out. Except for a very few, they did not really foresee, and consequently did not cope with, this shift. The epistemological and methodological self-critique that is raging in anthropology as a discipline now (however necessary and possibly healthy it may turn out to be) does not cope with this shift either, because the change is one in political or ideological attitudes, which are not seriously addressed. Again, anthropologists in the United States (more than in Europe, although new fashions are discussed here too) are exemplifying their marginality in the broader political arena in this respect. I will finish with an especially telling but rather superficial experience that may illustrate this point better.

In August 1990, we were on the Navajo reservation again. The Iraq crisis suddenly broke loose, and warlike speeches and analyses started pouring out of all the media. In record time, the military and political specialists invaded the news. Any democracy has the enormous privilege and responsibility to demand discussion and information about such important and dramatic events and about the choices to be made and the deliberations leading to those choices. However, not only was the news invaded almost entirely by warmongers but also a debate on the fundamental issues of American dominance, multicultural or unicultural world view, culture and historical-ladenness of values, and so on was excluded totally. Not one anthropologist came to the fore to at least modify the "evidence" on satanic or Hitlerite features of the enemy; neither did any one of them offer a viable alternative in terms of Arab culture or something along the lines of the trade we are all engaged in. Chances are that those who tried to raise these issues were not allowed on the air in the general warlike atmosphere at the time. The postwar period of February and March 1991 at least offered the opportunity to speak out in the newsletters and other publications of the discipline. The important issue of the future New World Order and its potential subordination of other cultures (with or without sympathy is here beside the point) to one dominant culture, or, alternatively, its attempt to recognize a multicultural world, did not hold the attention of the specialists in this field, including anthropologists. Nothing of their expertise was offered in the general debate. The ensuing censuring of the media was silently tolerated. Chomsky was cited and discussed vehemently by European intellectuals, among them anthropologists. Radio and television throughout Europe (except Great Britain) repeatedly invited social scientists, spanning the whole range from historians to anthropologists. To the best of my knowledge, this was not the case in the United States. Of course, Europe played a secondary role in the conflict and did even that in a subdued way. But this cannot explain the silence of the thinking community in the United States.

On the individual level, the shock and the feeling of uneasiness was so intense that on the plane back to Europe I felt I was not informed enough about the conflict to form an opinion about it. I had practically no news about Arab, European, or Russian positions. They were entirely absent in American media, and it took me two weeks of intense reading of French, English, German, and Belgian newspapers and other publications to be able to reach some nuanced understanding of what was going on. My experience while in the United States was one of extreme *depaysement* (the closest I can come in translation is "unearthliness"). I could only wonder what happened to the American intellectual.

NO CONCLUSION WILL DO

The request on the part of the editors of this volume was to have impressions by foreign anthropologists about their contacts with the United States. It is impossible to be complete or even decently representative in a short piece, based on impressions. My only excuse for sending it in, as it stands, is that impressions are what a thinking human being feeds on, even if he or she does not publish them regularly. I hope these few notes help the reader to recognize the foreigner in me and through that mirror image to gather at least some view of the self.

TWELVE

Gender Encounters in America: An Outsider's View of Continuity and Ambivalence

RAHEL WASSERFALL
Duke University

Professor Wasserfall describes coming to grips with gender encounters in the context of academic culture at a southern university. To inform her analysis, she draws on her background in both Israel and France. The author cogently illustrates how our fragmented society makes ambiguity in relationships problematic for Americans.

Rahel Wasserfall *is a visiting lecturer at the Institute of Sociology and Social Policy, Eotvos Lorand University of Budapest. She was born and raised in France and spent seventeen years living in Israel. As a Fulbright scholar, she visited for two years at Duke University in North Carolina. She received her B.A. in Philosophy and Sociology (1978) and her M.A. (1981) and Ph.D. (1987) in Social Anthropology and Sociology from the Hebrew University of Jerusalem.*

INTRODUCTION

In the following pages I will retrace my experiences with American culture as I encountered it in a college town in the south of the United States. The university where I was located is private and very prestigious; it is sometimes referred to as "the Harvard of the South." It was my first encounter with the States, where I had come to teach and pursue my research interests. As an anthropologist, I aim to understand others' ways of being human. One type of work that I believe can help us grasp this anthropological project focuses on revealing what things the persons in a culture take for granted. This emphasis on revealing the assumptions of what makes a culture seem "natural" for the "natives"—the things that are taken for granted—stems from the subject matter of the anthropological project itself: the relation between self and other.

The first few weeks in a new field are critical for understanding what is taken for granted. Because of the effect of one's own cultural displacement, one is most able to "see" what is for informants their "taken for granted" way of living and their assumptions about their cultural constructions. While still "living" cognitively in one's previous culture, one has to cope with the new setting, and in the first few weeks, one's "being" is in both cultures simultaneously. I believe that with the passing of time the first feelings, pregnant with meanings about the new culture, fade as one becomes accustomed to the new ways.

The first few weeks in a new country, although difficult and draining, are loaded with seeds of understanding. I found months later that impressions written in my daily journal of those days unfolded as insights pertaining to some cultural aspects of the American academia I encountered. These first impressions (often just feelings) must be followed by further rigorous observations, but in them lies an important tool for grasping contradictions, assumptions that bear on what I believe it means to understand another culture.

A sense of amazement mixed with fear were my common feelings in those first days. The language, the smells, and the smiles of American scholars were alien. Coming from Jerusalem where so many American scholars pass through every year, I thought I was familiar with Americans, but this was different! I was on their turf, and I was no more the hostess to my culture, very much attracted by "those Americans," whom I thought then had the analytical answers to so many theoretical questions I was struggling with.

CLASSIFICATIONS? WHICH KIND?

The first thing that amazed me, that struck me as different from Jerusalem, was the content of what mattered, of what was important in one's first encounters with Americans. In every culture, people need to know some information to establish any interaction; information is needed to know what to expect if a relationship is to develop. But the content and style of the categorization varies from culture to culture. For example, my Jewish Moroccan informants living in an Israeli Moshav wanted to know the origin of my family, but they avoided disclosing any information about their social and political position. My Israeli informants were maintaining a margin of security and did not reveal too much of who they were in our first encounters. The "who they were" that mattered in this specific encounter was occluded and shaped by ambivalence. People were not really telling each other what their intentions were beyond the context of the particular encounter. Many interpretations of this phenomenon can be proposed: Some people are linked to their difficult economic situation, some to their specific political organization, and some perhaps to the contradictory meanings and imperative of the evil eye and honor in their culture (Wasserfall 1987). In the American context, I found that although some information was wanted right away, its content and style differed from one setting to the next. Whereas in the Moshav the style of the encounter was blurred by ambiguity, in the American cultural context the information was to be given right away, without ambivalence and in a straightforward manner.

THE SCENE

The American scholars I knew in Israel behaved differently from the ones I met at the southern university. In America, they did not have time for anything; they were always running from one place to the other. I began to see that what they called "work" was the motor of their life. American scholars, who in the midst of Jerusalem's "hot" days had time to sit down, have a drink, a long talk on any subject, not always connected to their topic of inquiry, were, in their home base, no longer available. I found myself having to schedule lunches with people three weeks in advance. I struggled to find people to talk with, not because they were not willing to talk but because they had so many things to do. I recall one person, after having attended an all-day conference, asking me when we departed at 7 P.M., "Are you going to work tonight?" I was completely puzzled. Work? I just wanted to relax and think about what went on that day. I suddenly understood that work for my American friends has a larger meaning than it has for me. For me, "working" is when I am writing or when I am reading in connection to my ongoing interests. Attending a conference and talking with people is not work for me; for them it is! When my friends talk of seventy hours of work a week, they include everything they do, while for me most of these activities are not considered work.

With time, I began to wonder if this use of "work" has to do with the American need to classify everything in manageable boxes. I was puzzled by the work ethic. I wanted to understand what this meant: Did they really "work" all the time? Did they want to impress me? Did they want to impress each other? All these may, in some cases, be true, but I finally came to believe that this use of work was not an excuse to protect their intimacy or their time but in effect bore on their way of classifying their reality and themselves. Work is used as a metaphor for stating one's sense of worth and identity in the competitive world of academia. I would even venture to say that work takes a role akin to that of honor among my Jewish Moroccan informants as a vehicle of identity formation. In my circle of American academics, "work" was the way to shape and state their identity as adult members of American society.¹ Work was a way to classify reality. When an event was classified as work, it was presented as legitimate and seen as a positive way to pursue one's unfolding sense of identity—unfolding in the sense that one's identity is very precarious and depends on outside gratification to be realized. One has to fight, to struggle to keep one's identity as a member of the American academic setting (where stories of failure and rejections of "successful" scholars are told as alcove secrets). Work, in this fragmented reality, has a very important role; it makes things clear and gives one's identity "presence."

Work, as a metaphor for classifying one's self in a fragmented reality (imbuing it with a sense of core identity), is a powerful tool to classify one's sense of worth and self. But this need for clear, unambiguous definitions of reality is also the style I found in gender encounters with my American friends. They dealt with possible romance in a business-like way. In a romance relation, one constructs not only his or her own sense of self but also its perception of or by the other.

ARE YOU FREE?

I am a French-born woman who immigrated to Israel in her late teens. I lived seventeen years in Israel, and I was thirty-four when I came to the university alone (my partner having moved at that time from Israel to Los Angeles). I was meeting people in the context of my eagerness to learn more about this place and about its intellectual life. After a few encounters with men and women in the community, I realized that before talking "work" or "business," which was the topic of our coming together, I was very subtly asked or told something that I would label "private," not belonging in the arena of work. These sentences always were about their marital or private life situation and mine as well.

For example, I was meeting a male anthropologist who was about my age, and we were on our way to have lunch. Almost immediately he said something about going with his wife to Washington over the weekend. I myself found a way to answer a few sentences later that, "I will be going to visit my partner in L.A. next month." After this (in my view) strange dialogue, we went on talking about anthropology and his interests. I was struck. Why did he have to mention his wife a few minutes after we had met? Did I give him some kind of sexual cues? Did he see this encounter in romantic tones? Why did I have to mention my partner? What was even more interesting is that after having told each other that we were in stable relationships, we were able to enjoy each other's company on a collegial level. I found this peculiar but did not think about the matter, until I had another meeting with another colleague and something similar happened. I began to be intrigued and asked myself, Do I send sexual messages to men? Is something about my behavior wrong? Is my style, my clothing, or my

French accent the "problem"? Then I met a woman who told me that she was gay and that she was "open" to any kind of a relationship. I talked about my partner, and we then established a friendship. Repeatedly, people I had just met were eager to let me know where they stood in their personal lives and they wanted to learn about my position, too. I found myself giving away this information easily, as a way to establish contact with a new person, with a new "other." I learned that men and women alike, when confronted with a new person, wanted to know certain characteristics and not others. They knew from the start that I was an anthropologist, female, and French-Israeli. However, it emerged that what they wanted to know was not my class, my kin, my religious or political beliefs, or the origin of my family but my marital situation—and they had to know it as soon as possible!

I believe that in any encounter, in any culture, people need *some* information to feel comfortable, but I am wondering why one's marital situation became an issue in a context defined as work, when work, as I noted previously, is presented as so important and salient in the lives of my American friends.

AMBIGUITY AND AMBIVALENCE

I was discussing this issue with an American friend, a university professor. She recalled the following story about her personal life. A man she was interested in did not tell her that he was married while, at the same time, making strong indications of a romantic interest in her. She learned quickly (through common acquaintances) that this person was married. My friend became very angry and ended her relationship with him. She later learned that this man was in the midst of a divorce. (He subsequently became involved with a friend of hers, whom he married soon after getting his divorce.) While listening to my impressions about American gender encounters, she was struck by her own style. My friend wanted to know the man's marital status right away, whereas he, for various reasons, could not tell her. She got angry and did not let any romantic feelings develop between them. She needed to know as soon as possible what his position was, and she interpreted his not telling her as a bad character trait.

When my friend told me this story, I recalled how French men and women interact. When you have a drink with a colleague, your marital status is never broached, and people enjoy the ambivalence of the situation, the possible flirtation even if no one is interested in starting a relationship. I asked myself how much information I actually knew about my French colleagues. More important, when in our relationship did I learn about their personal lives? For my French colleagues, it took a long time before I was told their personal histories. In France, people will "let things happen"; in America, there seems to be no time, no room for "letting things happen." From the first encounter on, one has to know if this relationship could lead to something and what kind of potential there is. Very little room is left for ambiguity, to slowly find out about the person, to let your imagination wonder about what you do not yet know. I believe this ambiguous style is at the basis of any encounter between genders in France, whereas in the American context, ambiguity is not well coped with and is interpreted as an untrustworthy character trait.[2]

My American friends were interested in letting me know what their personal situations were, and they wanted to know, as soon as possible, what my situation was. I was puzzled: How can one "fall in love" when things are so tailored? As I became acquainted with more people, it struck me that the uneasiness with ambiguity can be seen in other parts of their lives, for example in their ways of "processing information" (see below). Is this related to the American need to be in control or to their "instrumental" rationality? How is the self/other relationship perceived and constructed in American academic culture?

PROCESSING INFORMATION

In the first month of my stay at the university, I was overwhelmed by feelings, situations, and new people. I had to make sense of all these new situations. My journals from those days are full of the uses of "processing information." My American friends were trying to help me by giving me advice on how to "process information," how to put feelings into boxes—in Hochschild's (1985) terms "how to manage one's heart." I was telling a friend about an encounter I had at the grocery store. It was a bad day. I was not very focused and did not succeed in writing my check correctly. The clerk was very puzzled, since I looked "normal." She asked, "You do not know how to write a check? My god, where are you from?" I said something about being French (I did not want her to label my Israeli identity in a negative way, in an embarrassing situation). My friend tried to make me see how this information matched my research interest on identity. From her point of view everything had to be explained, thus contextualizing and delineating all experience (and legitimizing feelings, I might add) in terms of data.

In the first weeks of my stay, I went through some difficult times, which is the way I generally experience a new field situation. I was immediately labeled as "depressed." I was told that this behavior of mine is not "constructive" and that people are not going to like what they are seeing. I rapidly understood that my inner feelings of loss and despair at being in a new place and having to cope with so many problems at once were of no interest. A good anthropologist was expected to cope in a professional manner and have the skills to process all this information. The way I handled this situation was my rite of passage into their society. If I succeeded, I would prove that I am a good anthropologist;

if I failed, my skills as an anthropologist would be questioned. I listened to the power relations at work and actually did succeed in adapting, in showing a smiling face, but at the price of not being able to grasp the feelings I had in those few weeks. Now I wonder if perhaps in this "adaptation" I have lost some keys to understanding American society (Storper-Perez and Wasserfall 1988). There is no cultural room for anguish, fear, angst, or ambiguity here. Those are topics one deals with in the privacy of therapy.

WHY NOT AMBIVALENCE?

Sensitivity to ambiguity is different from sensitivity to pluralism. American culture, at least in academia, accepts pluralism as a value where being able to show the different points of view is a skill very much appreciated in scholarship. But pluralism is not ambivalence. While pluralism, as a value, implies a legitimation of different life-styles, ambiguity is an inner state where one is willing to cope with an undefined situation. I found that in a setting where pluralism becomes a moral imperative, one needs more and more information and takes less and less knowledge of his or her interlocutor for granted. For example, I was in the late stage of my pregnancy when I met a new colleague at a lecture, and we decided to have lunch. When we were waiting to be seated, my obvious pregnancy became the focus of her kindly interest. She asked if I had a coach (meaning someone to help me in childbirth). I answered affirmatively, and her next question was about the gender of my coach. I laughed and told her, "The father of my child is my coach." This colleague of mine wanted to know very rapidly some kind of information about me.

I was definitively pregnant, but she did not assume this meant that I was in a stable relationship or that the father of the child was also my partner. She did not take anything for granted. My bulging belly did not mean anything about my marital situation or sexual preference. To be able to negotiate relationships in the pluralistic world she lives in, she had to know immediately where I stood. I believe that in a pluralistic society, where the rules of interaction are changing rapidly, one has to learn quickly where his or her interlocutor stands, not only not to offend them but also to be able to relate at all. In such a context, ambiguity will make a person very uncomfortable because not knowing how to relate, to bargain, and to build that necessary sense of continuity interferes with the negotiation of identity in a fragmented society. For my Israeli informants, ambiguity is a style of interaction because of the stability of most parts of their lives and the need in such conditions to protect their social and political bargaining. From this experience, it would seem that the way a culture deals with ambiguity resonates with the ways self-identity is constructed in that society.

THE RELATION BETWEEN SELF-IDENTITY
AND THE OTHER: CONTINUITY AND AMBIGUITY

The construction of identity is a dialectical pendulum, swinging between personal action and public recognition (Berger and Luckman 1967). On the theoretical level, there is a dialectic of limit and continuity, both in reciprocal relationship. I take the position that identity is to be understood through the concept of limit. Limit and continuity are the two elements through which identity is shaped, limit being the constraints and the boundaries within which certain kinds of choices (within the continuity of a given cultural tradition) are possible (Wasserfall 1987). Continuity transcends limits between social categories and generations (such as being Jewish, a woman, Israeli). However, the imposition of limits breaks continuities between insiders and outsiders, and one acquires a sense of self by understanding what one is not, that is, what one is limited from (such as not being an American, a woman, a man, an Arab).

Identification occurs through the Other.[3] A culture can focus on the Other (difference) or on continuities between individuals in the process of identity formation. When a culture focuses on the Other, as I believe the Israeli-Moroccan culture does, limits appear as a fundamental notion of cultural identity. In reference to the Other, people in that culture extract and impose limits on their own behavior and on the behavior of others. But when a culture focuses on the self and individuality, as American culture does, continuity becomes important. In this context one finds a dislike for ambiguous situations, and ambivalence in romantic situations is not tolerated. Ambiguity and ambivalence blur the continuity needed to grasp one's identity in a fragmented modern situation.

American academe is a pluralistic milieu where one is aware of cultural, social, racial and sexual differences. In such a context, rules of interaction are not set, and one needs a clear style of interaction to cope with these conditions. Here, I have presented, albeit tentatively, the importance my American interlocutors place on nonambiguity as an outcome of their focus on the fragmentation of their lives and the need for continuity. I am suggesting that American academics, when dealing with the relation between self and a gendered other (in a context defined as heterosexual or homosexual), need to define rigorously and unambiguously what other cultures (at least the two I am familiar with) regard as a whimsical feeling: romance. As a concept, continuity is the content of one's sense of self, which, in a fragmented milieu, must be constructed as a stable component.

Continuity, as an aspect of identity, has both a cognitive and a behavioral aspect. Seeking continuity on the behavioral level, as well as on the symbolic level, is a way to manipulate and bargain for one's own identity while simultaneously establishing the other's identity. This is especially true in a fragmented context where pluralism is a moral imperative.

In this paper I have taken a specific role as participant observer, but I am also an academic and a woman. I have tried to recall my coming to terms with some parts of my experience as a woman in academia. I believe that the uneasiness found with ambiguity is best seen in the "struggle" to master romantic feelings in gender encounters. This reluctance to live with ambiguity may be linked to the importance of continuity in a process of identity construction in a fragmented context where rules of interaction are changing.

NOTES

1. This is in concordance with some of the arguments put forward by Smelser and Erickson (1980) in their edited volume, *Themes of Work and Love in Adulthood,* Harvard University Press.

2. That the issue of one's marital situation does not come up often in Israel is perhaps because Israelis assume that after a certain age one is in a stable relationship and has children.

3. I extracted the concept of limit from the discussions of both Lévi-Strauss and Benoist in the seminar conducted by Lévi-Strauss in 1974–1975.

REFERENCES

BERGER, PETER, AND THOMAS LUCKMANN
1967   The Social Construction of Reality: A Treatise in the Sociology of Knowledge. New York: Doubleday.

HOCHSCHILD, ARLIE R.
1985   The Managed Heart: Commercialization of Human Feelings. Berkeley: University of California Press.

STORPER-PEREZ, DANIELLE, AND RAHEL WASSERFALL
1988   Methodologie de la Raison, Methodologie de la Resonnance. Revue de L'Institut de Sociologie. Universite Libre de Bruxelles, Belgique (1–2): 189–207.

WASSERFALL, RAHEL
1987   Gender Identification in an Israeli Moshav. Ph.D. dissertation (December). Hebrew University of Jerusalem.

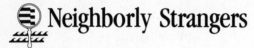 Neighborly Strangers

HONGGANG YANG

Carter Center, Emory University

Honggang Yang spent two years doing fieldwork in a private cluster homes neighborhood in Florida. In this essay he focuses on how American homeowners both resist and come to terms with the ownership of common property by contrasting his experience in Florida to his experience in urban China. He clearly articulates the barriers that American individualism creates for the development of community among his neighbors in "Pondtrees."

Honggang Yang is a research associate in Conflict Resolution Programs at the Carter Center of Emory University. He had medical training in undergraduate education and studied social psychology in graduate school in China. Before coming to the United States in 1986, Honggang Yang was a faculty member in the Department of Sociology at Nankai University. He was the 1989/1990 National Champion of a scholarship essay competition for international students. He earned his Ph.D. in Applied Anthropology at the University of South Florida in 1991. Dr. Yang's research interests are in the fields of legal anthropology, community organizations, and management of common property resources.

I spent almost two years doing fieldwork in an American neighborhood with a homeowners association. My ethnographic curiosity is about how American homeowners in a private cluster homes development share and manage common property resources, such as neighborhood fences, swimming pools, tennis courts, picnic sites, parking lots, entrance areas, playgrounds, and clubhouses. Like many anthropologists engaged in fieldwork overseas, I was often puzzled by the foreign patterns of social relations in this modern residential corporation in the United States, since I had grown up in China where communal life was quite different. At the beginning of my field endeavor, I could not see the "problems" in what were considered problems by my informants, and I could not understand why what I perceived as problems were not regarded as "problems" by the residents.

In my writings, I call my field site "Pondtrees"—a fictitious name. Pondtrees is located in a suburb of the Tampa Bay area. The development was started in the mid-1970s and completed in the early 1980s. There are now about five hundred homes in Pondtrees. As the place name indicates, there are several ponds and lakes and plenty of trees. The development has two kinds of homes: the single-family house or detached building and the townhome or contiguous unit. The larger lake in the area serves as a marker: All of the single-family homes are on the west side of the lake, whereas most of the townhomes are on the east shore. However, homeowners of both groups are mandatory members of the association. There are also a considerable number of absentee homeowners and renters in Pondtrees.

When I started fieldwork, I was first struck by the legalistic and commercial multiplicity of the residential organization. In Pondtrees, homeowners are obligated to pay dues to the association for maintaining the common facilities and common areas. Owners of townhomes pay more because they receive more services like pest control, mowing, roofing, siding, and repairing exterior parts of their property. The board of directors, consisting of five volunteers elected from among the homeowners, contracts a property manager to do the jobs. A set of documents are the legal basis for the operation and governance of the association. The highly specialized rules and regulations for Pondtrees are contained in documents entitled Restated Articles of Incorporation; Bylaws; Restated Declaration of Easements, Covenants, Conditions, and Restrictions; Master Declarations; and Townhome Declarations. I was astonished by the complexity as well as the quantity of the collection. There are a multitude of signatures and stamps on the documents, imprints of approval and witness. In one of the documents, the Restated Declaration, there are at least twenty-three signatures and seven stamps.

Pondtrees is quiet. Residents are seldom well acquainted with one another, in sharp contrast to my residence in China where every neighbor knows each other. In the Chinese urban neighborhood where my parents still reside, the residential setting and communal atmosphere appear characteristic of *Gemeinschaft* (traditional community). Residents in such a community are often employed in the same work unit. There exists ongoing mutual aid among neighbors, which includes watching the stove, buying vegetables, helping move furniture, and taking care of children for each other. As a child, I customarily addressed my neighbors in senior generations by the kinship terms *uncle* or *aunt*.

Different from the American counterpart, urban houses in China are usually not privately owned but are provided by the government through work units. Migration into cities is restricted, unless one is recruited by the government. Urban residents are all legally required to register to gain jobs, housing, food, health care, school, and the like. The neighborhood is geographically bounded, consisting of several adjacent blocks with from a hundred to a few hundred households. There is a resident committee in each neighborhood, which is a semiautonomous multifunctional organization. I call it "semi" because of its political affiliation with the party and state and its folk ties with local residents. It is organizationally different from the board of directors of American homeowners associations in many ways. In China, the committee members are chosen or elected from among volunteers, most of whom are retired elders and housewives with charismatic authority carrying social respect, credit, and trust. They assist the local government in conducting household registration, inspecting block sanitation, supervising individual immunizations, family planning, handling minor criminal cases, mediating civil and domestic disputes, coordinating a neighborhood watch, and holding some social activities.

While my family and I were in Pondtrees, my wife often expressed to me her personal reactions to the neighborhood. She sometimes complained that our immediate neighbors never invited her over to chat, visit, or have supper together. I remember that last year when we were moving from one house to another within Pondtrees, my wife intended to look for help from the neighbors and wished that someone had given us a hand.

Undoubtedly, the prevalence of high residential mobility in U.S. society is a factor contributing to the existing lack of communal sentiment. Around my house in the townhome section, there are several adjacent buildings with four units each. My neighbors change almost constantly, moving in and out. There are quite a few vacant units, and on several are signs of "For Sale" or "Assumable Owner." I found that residents rarely get to know each other. One of my informants in the single-family section told me that his next-door neighbors have changed three times in the past two years. But my fieldwork experience also taught me that most of the residents do not have intentions or expectations to know each other beyond saying hello in the street. Some of them believe that Pondtrees is simply a place to live; others consider it an investment; still a few of them refer to it as a "community." Despite the cognitive differences, they always seem ready to move.

I describe the residents in Pondtrees as "neighborly strangers." "Neighborly" used here has two meanings, one referring to the physical vicinity or the spatial contiguity of their residence and another connoting a routine presentation of self as "nice." A good neighbor in this context is expected to be "friendly" with others, rather than a friend. "Strangers" implies the remote interpersonal distances among the neighbors, as distinct from my neighbors in China, who not only know each other's ages, occupations, ranks, economic conditions, family histories, relatives, and personal hobbies but also often offer help. My neighbors in Pondtrees, on the other hand, seldom have that kind of knowledge and trust, since such knowledge may entail a sort of invasion of privacy. Their shelters are too close to allow them to be friends in such a living domain, perhaps due to what I term "privacy considerations." My wife once commented that maintaining surface interaction without a greater sense of community was almost meaningless, and it would lead to feelings of uncertainty and indifference among neighbors. Not having neighbors as friends doesn't mean that the residents have no friends but that they make friends somewhere else. When I approached the residents, asking questions about neighborhood concerns, they often responded very briefly with common expressions of "You know what I mean" or "You know what I am saying." They seemed reluctant to talk more and were politely on guard. There seems to exist an invisible interpersonal boundary that is almost impossible for "nonfriends" to penetrate.

The mobile and anonymous conditions of life in Pondtrees significantly affect the harmony of communal life. The neighborhood atmosphere is sometimes marred by the prevalent apathetic attitudes and frequent complaints about the commons shared and managed by residents themselves. One informant, who had been vice president of the board, told me his experience: "No matter what you do, everybody hates you." While I was in the field, I attended every monthly board meeting, and there were only about a dozen participants. I was surprised at the beginning because I expected more residents to be active in their neighborhood. One of my informants told me that low attendance is a good sign that means fewer complaints and less trouble. Later, I found that my informant was right about those who came to the meetings. Most of the participants usually have ideas, concerns, confusions, problems, or issues on the maintenance and services. For example, some of the common complaints were about the inconsistent decorative colors of homes, curtains, windows, and fences, which in my eyes could have been ignored. Typically, there are more complaints than constructive suggestions about the commons in the neighborhood, and there are fewer residents willing to volunteer for the board or committees than critics. For several consecutive years, the annual meeting, the most important activity of the association (election, budgets, and finance), could not reach a quorum and had to hold a second meeting with a lower quorum.

In Pondtrees, I presented myself as a resident as well as a student, and I volunteered in quite a few ways to get more involved. For example, I served as a clubhouse coordinator. One day when I was on duty at the clubhouse, I found an interesting newspaper clipping titled "Motto":

Stay away from meetings. If you come, find fault and never offer an alternative. Decline office or appointment to a committee. Get sore if you aren't nominated.

After you are nominated, don't attend board or committee meetings. If you get to one, despite your better judgment, clam up until you get outside, then sound off on how things should have been done.

Don't work if you can avoid it. When the old reliables pitch in, accuse them of being a clique.

Oppose all banquets, parties, seminars, conferences, and trade missions as being a waste of the attendees' money. If everything is strictly business, then complain that the meetings are dull and officers belong to the old guard.

Never accept a place at the head table. If you aren't asked to sit there, threaten to resign because you aren't appreciated.

Don't rush to pay your dues; let the directors sweat—after all, they wrote the budget. Read the mail from the association only now and then; never reply if you can help it, and then ask why you were not informed.

This "motto" is an exaggerated depiction of some common dilemmas involving sharing in such an environment. It reflects, in a dramatic way, an embedded contradiction between the individual and the commons. The essence of the commons is to provide resources that are needed but are difficult or impossible to provide individually. I asked some of my informants for their comments on the "motto." They told me that it was true but varied per particular individual, for a particular period of time, on a particular issue, and in a particular context. The cynical attitudes in the "motto" expressed implicit tension and disharmony, and these attitudes were, in fact, not less influential in neighborhood life than apathy. Neither the cynicism nor the apathy, in my opinion, are constructive or healthy.

There were also occasional legal battles that reflected another aspect of the neighborhood—communal politics and interpersonal tension in Pondtrees. About two years ago, a number of the homeowners found that a board member was delinquent in his monthly dues but was somehow permitted to take part in the association election at the annual meeting. This incident happened at the time when a controversial, extraordinary assessment was proposed by the board. The dissatisfied homeowners decided to hire an attorney to sue the board of directors for permitting the board member to vote. According to the Bylaws, homeowners failing to pay assessments prior to the meeting are not entitled to enjoy the benefit of association membership, including electing and getting elected. But the tricky part of the dispute centered around the fact that the delinquent board member submitted a check for payment just before the meeting and then requested that the check be returned to him the following day because he was not financially able to meet his obligation. To defend the stand taken, the board also sought legal counsel from the association attorney. The association attorney held that the board's permission was legally legitimate and did not influence the voting.

Facing such legal threats and possible court action, the board of directors decided to indemnify its members, which meant spending additional money on buying insurance—a guarantee against personal liability in conjunction with board service in the nonprofit corporation. This episode illustrates a painful and complex aspect of the usually quiet situations in Pondtrees. It reveals that going to court more or less becomes one of the standard facts of communal life in a neighborhood like Pondtrees. This whole issue perplexed me. I thought that life in an American suburban common property development would be peaceful and economical. To achieve harmony, however, the residents need to work to solve their problems while maintaining communal unity.

In China, neighborhood mediation is one of the distinctive functions of the resident committee, and it is characterized by an informal, decentralized, self-governing approach on a face-to-face basis at the grass-roots level. Under the state ownership of housing and with the dominance of the cultural value of kinship, not many residents concern themselves with the maintenance of the common resources they share or other nonkinship, public matters. These are the recurrent problems and issues in such scenes. The inside of individual homes may be tidy and in good order, but the shared areas like corridors and entrances are sometimes messy and vandalized. In such cases, the committee members will approach the responsible residents directly, explain the problem, and persuade them to correct it. Conflict resolution within the neighborhood remains relatively undifferentiated between communal matters and family affairs. For example, if a couple has a big quarrel and one of them seeks a divorce, the neighbors who hear it may tell the committee members and then the committee members may mediate between the two sides, reminding them of the happiness of their marriage and helping them understand each other in that emotional situation. This pattern of neighborhood dispute resolution correlates with the emphasis on "harmony of life" in Chinese culture as well as with the socioeconomic context where urban mobility is low.

Even in Pondtrees, against the background of apathy and cynicism, there has been a successful community organization operating without interruption—the garden club. It came into being on the partial completion of the development and is still running. It demonstrates the convergence of individual interests and communal benefits. Every home has a courtyard, and greenery is found throughout Pondtrees. Either the individual or the association must take care of the gardens, yards, and common areas one way or another. Also, the increasing environmental awareness in society reinforces the positive perceptions of the role of this organization.

Basically, the garden club is autonomously organized for the informal exchange of ideas, information, and help in the maintenance and beautification of the surroundings within individual courtyards or in front of homes. Starting with some individual horticultural hobbies, the club extended its activities to natural preservation and neighborhood landscaping in Pondtrees. It was loosely organized, so there was little pressure. It served as a popular arena for residents' interests and provided some enjoyable labor for members in their leisure time. The club activists responded to my curiosity about its success with "We just love doing it." The club introduced plants and shrubbery suitable for the soil and seasons and managed to get a good deal for the plants. They also offered their expertise and made recommendations to the association and individual residents for the selection of plants both in the common areas and in individual backyards. The club also invited local speakers for water, land, and other natural conservation campaigns and helped distribute the information.

Although there is a separate committee in charge of landscaping in Pondtrees, the tasks are sometimes closely combined with those of the club. In the last two years, the garden club has selected four "Yard-of-the-Month" designations. The award is based on overall attractiveness and improvement and is intended to recognize and honor those promoting natural beautification on their property and in Pondtrees. The selection goes on smoothly except that two of the honorary signs were once stolen. These special efforts improve the communal atmosphere while contributing to community formation, and some of the residents even purchase plants for the common areas. Quite a few of the club members volunteered for other neighborhood committees and later got elected to the board of directors. To my surprise the other day, I saw one of my neighbors (renting in the building next to mine) taking care of the plants in the common area the day before he moved out of Pondtrees.

The homeowners association in Pondtrees is a fascinating sociocultural and economic construct. I find that the management of common property by the residents themselves shows a convergence of individualism and volunteerism, although there exist ambiguities concerning the commons, leading to a variety of disharmonies and conflicts. Individualism is a way that people look at and are adapted to their world. An individualistic worldview considers the individual as the elementary unit of primary order, whereas society is viewed as a secondary or artificial construct.

Like any other cultural value, individualism is effective only in some contexts. In some ways it is liable to produce alienation. I see individualism as a reaction to the constraints of society and nature that tries to solve the contradictions between self and the outside world by assigning primary importance to the individual. Residing in a neighborhood with a homeowners association entails cooperating and sharing, which is sometimes incongruent with American ideals of individuality and independence. American individualism is quite like a two-edged sword: on the one edge, trying to gain something always pursued, such as individual freedom and happiness; on the other, taking a risk of losing something still needed, such as a trusting human community and togetherness.

Compared with the community life in my Chinese neighborhood, interpersonal relations among neighbors in Pondtrees were aloof, cold, and lacking of an expectation for future interaction. However, human problems and issues are ubiquitous and embedded in sociocultural institutions. Furthermore, communal life indeed varies in different societal structures. Both Chinese and American cultures have their weaknesses and shortcomings as well as their strengths and advantages. The headaches suffered by my Chinese neighbors were different from the complaints expressed by my American neighbors in Pondtrees. I believe that the neighborly strangers in my neighborhood could benefit by becoming more aware of their common ground and communal needs, while the quality of life in my Chinese community could be enhanced by overcoming institutionalized political and economic barriers and sociocultural weak points. After all, we are transients, as Chinese-American anthropologist F. L. K. Hsu points out, and what we need is a pleasant journey through this world. We should try our best to gain benefits from cross-cultural knowledge and to be free from those physical and psychological sufferings existent in both of our cultures.

ACKNOWLEDGMENTS

I am grateful to Professors A. W. Wolfe, M. V. Angrosino, S. D. Greenbaum, J. E. Jreisat, and E. G. Nesman for their direction and comments during my studying and writing at University of South Florida. I am also thankful to Ron Habin for his editorial assistance.

FOURTEEN

A European Anthropologist's Personal and Ethnographic Impressions of the United States

EMANUEL J. DRECHSEL
University of Hawai'i at Mānoa

In this wide-ranging and personal essay, Professor Drechsel discusses the American penchant for viewing ourselves as culturally European. Using his European background and long-term familiarity with the United States, he argues convincingly that there is a unique American culture strongly influenced by non-European sources, especially the Native American culture. For the author, this culture includes elements of a Wild West mentality but is best understood as a "creole" in which non-European elements are not always obvious or distinct. He concludes the essay by offering the compelling comparison of American culture to a circus.

Emanuel J. Drechsel *was born and raised in Switzerland. He studied anthropology with a focus on Native American languages of the eastern United States and received a Ph.D. from the University of Wisconsin-Madison in 1979. He has lived and done anthropological research (including fieldwork) in the upper Midwest, the South (especially Louisiana), and Hawai'i. Married to a native Hawaiian, he currently resides in Honolulu and is an associate professor of Liberal Studies at the University of Hawai'i at Mānoa.*

INTRODUCTION

The careers of anthropologists, as those of other professionals, reveal distinctly personal dimensions and reflect such diverse influences as individual experiences, sociocultural roots or a certain disillusionment with them, and often an interest of a romantic nature. Such individual traits are evident in biographies of two intellectual ancestors of mine,

Wilhelm von Humboldt (Sweet 1978/1980) and *Edward Sapir: Linguist, Anthropologist, Humanist* (Darnell 1990), as in those of other scholars. Accordingly, I have always been aware of a distinct personal dimension in my own career as an anthropologist and linguist and in my perspective as a foreigner living in the United States. My sociocultural background and personal experiences not only explain my areas of interest and even my reasons for coming to the United States but obviously have also colored my views of this country.[1]

Thus, examining the personal backgrounds of anthropologists— particularly the backgrounds of foreign anthropologists—is an important part of understanding their professional views. Such a review is warranted for reasons no less significant than realizing their presumptions, misconceptions, and even prejudices, for the recognition of any personal bias can help both the anthropologists and others to revise their understandings of a foreign society. Yet, beyond this basic reason, there is another justification—perhaps equally important but rarely recognized explicitly—for considering the personal dimensions in anthropologists' perspectives, experiences, and observations. Anthropologists' personal experiences not only may reveal the subjectivity and limits of their observations, but also may provide different angles and serve as inspiration for new ideas that a native might ignore or miss. In short, the anthropologists' personal backgrounds may add—so to speak—twists to their observations, with positive as well as negative consequences.

To help the reader unwind any "personal twists" in my observations below, I first offer an autobiographical sketch including information on my upbringing, sociocultural background, and personal experiences. These, I contend, relate directly to my experiences as a foreign anthropologist in the United States, even if such a connection may first appear insignificant. What follows leads to an informal account of personal impressions and ethnographic observations I have made as a European in this country. They specifically consist of personal experiences, informal observations in and out of the classroom, systematic fieldwork with Native Americans and other ethnic groups, and ethnohistorical research over a period of some twenty years.[2]

ROOTS, UPBRINGING, AND YOUTH

I was born in Switzerland in 1949 and grew up in the northeastern part in a little town by the name of Romanshorn, located on the Lake of Constance in the canton of Thurgau. My mother and her side of the family have always reminded me in a kind of ancestor's myth that we were Appenzellers, descendants of small but sturdy peasants in the hills and mountains south of the lake, recognized for many "peculiar" traditions among other Swiss. Descent has indeed tied my family to a small community in the half-canton of Appenzell Outer-Rhoden through my mother's father, who, however, was the only immediate ancestor with ties to northeastern Switzerland.

In reality, I can maintain little claim to an Appenzeller identity, for I never met my maternal grandfather, apparently a most remarkable man, who had unfortunately died before I was born. Significantly, he had not even lived in his native canton, nor has anybody else in my immediate family for that matter. My mother's mother had roots in French-speaking Switzerland and in France. A maternal aunt, my mother's oldest sister, always presented herself as American, as she had settled in the United States as a young woman. On my father's side, I have had roots in Germany, about which I have never learned many details but some of which supposedly extended even farther to Sweden and Russia. As a boy, I also acquired ties to the United States through my American godfather, who eventually married my mother. An inspiring model and a gentleman in the truest sense of the word, he has always enjoyed my admiration, for he never assumed the role of a stereotypical stepfather and—sociologically speaking—has always remained more of a magnanimous uncle with his calm, nonimposing manners than an authority figure.

There is even less of a justification for an Appenzeller identity on a social basis, for my family has shown little sympathy for one of the Appenzellers' characteristic traditions, their long-lasting resistance to granting full political rights to women. (These rights were finally installed in the last holdout of institutionalized male predominance, Appenzell Inner-Rhoden, by a recent order of the Swiss federal court.) Although not exactly feminists by modern standards, the women in my family on the maternal side have always been quite independent and have pursued their own goals and careers, far more so than average Swiss, let alone Appenzeller, women. In the 1920s, my mother's mother, although not an architect, designed her own house, which has stood out because of its simple beauty. My maternal aunts likewise distinguished themselves in one fashion or another. One was among the first women in Switzerland to acquire a driver's license at a time when only men were behind the wheel. But, instead of turning into a "car freak," she became engaged in promoting public transportation and environmental protection when few people had even heard of ecology. Most important, my mother developed her own business designing and manufacturing jewelry, for which she won several national awards, and successfully switched to health therapy after "retirement."

Indeed, I grew up with little exposure to Appenzeller traditions. My only familiarity with Appenzell has been from sporadic hikes and skiing trips into the nearby mountains, which lead up to the dominant peak known as Säntis with a height of some 8,200 feet, clearly visible from my hometown on a nice day. But I have found mountains with all their imposing beauty as rather confining my horizon literally as well as metaphorically—not to mention that I remember mountains as the prime location of natural disasters in Switzerland (avalanches, floods, and earth slides). Since youth, I have also taken exception to the widespread Heidi mentality of identifying Switzerland with the Alps, especially the Matterhorn and the Lucerne areas that the Swiss tourist and other industries have much promoted. I have further objected to the accompanying philosophy of political conservatism as reflected in the Wilhelm Tell mentality of the mountain cantons[3] and as revealed again in recent disclosures of an unconstitutional underground branch of the Swiss army in the mountains. Counter to the common cliché, Switzerland has been much more than a beautiful rock in the midst of Europe, fine chocolate, handy army knives, precision watches, or secret bank accounts (see Gonseth 1989–1990).

The major geological landmark of my native country, the Alps, has thus had little positive emotional significance for me. For my home, I have always preferred the shore of the Lake of Constance with the adjacent lowlands and hills, the primary environment of my childhood. My emotional association with the lake has remained so strong that today I have retained few early memories, happy or sad, in which the lake does not figure if only in the background; in contrast, the mountains simply do not figure in my recollections, except for two or three. My orientation has thus been away from the mountains, that is, northward and northwestward, which also included a regular glimpse beyond Switzerland's national borders into the neighboring Federal Republic of Germany (FRG) or nearby Austria. A ferry has connected my native town, Romanshorn, with Friedrichshafen, the home of the first zeppelins. Once vehicles to the wide world, they flew again overseas to America in my imagination, inspired by old photographs and by my aunt's memories.

My multinational roots exposed me to things foreign in my early youth. My German father, an engineer by profession, acquainted me with different technologies—at first cars and trains, then redesigned sailing ships and windmills as examples of an alternative, ecologically responsible industry. He warned me of nuclear energy, environmental disasters without national borders (as in the case of Chernobyl), and fascism, which he had experienced personally.

My horizon widened literally as well as metaphorically when, as a teenager, I moved to Basel, the country's second largest city, located on the Rhine River in northern Switzerland in a triangular corner facing France and the Federal Republic of Germany. The river not only draws much of its water from the Lake of Constance but has also been Switzerland's major lifeline to the world at large. Because of its unique infrastructure, Basel has long been a center of transportation, industrialization, and international financing in Switzerland and has enjoyed a rich tradition of culture and education. The city also forms the heart of a larger international area known as *Regio Basiliensis* (Latin for "Basel region"), a socio-economic area that extends across national boundaries from northern Switzerland into the Alsace (France) and

Baden (FRG) and is bordered by the Jura and Vosges mountains and the Black Forest. This region has been the home of more than two million people sharing traditions in a common dialect, literature, architecture, and other characteristics and has successfully pursued across-the-border trinational cooperation independent of farther-reaching efforts at European economic and political integration such as the European Free Trade Association (EFTA) and the European Community (EC).

The reason for my move to Basel was to attend *Gymnasium* (an institution of secondary education equivalent to high school and at least the first few years of college) and later the university. I could conveniently join my stepfather, who as editor of the English magazine of a major pharmaceutical company was professionally engaged in this city during much of the week and maintained an apartment there. Through him and his American, British, and Anglophile Swiss friends, I acquired a taste and fascination for Anglo-Saxon "things," ranging from technology (such as the caboose at the tail of American freight trains, airplanes, sky scrapers, and suspension bridges) to food (like peanut butter, pumpkin pies, pancakes, and sandwiches). With a growing appreciation for Baroque and classical music, I learned to relish modern "serious" American music in the form of blues and jazz, which resounded from Basel's concert halls, museums, and smaller establishments. Jazz concerts during these years, such as the big-band swing by Count Basie and Duke Ellington, the cool music by the Modern Jazz Quartet, and free-jazz experimentations by Don Cherry, have remained part of my cherished memory until today. I even adopted some "Anglo-Saxon" mannerisms such as carrying change loosely in my pocket instead of in a wallet and wearing white socks with dark long pants (only to shock some Americans with my "low-class" attire years later on my first visit to the United States). Moreover, I identified my stepfather's calm and relaxed manners as characteristically American and also eyed smoking the pipe as an expression of Anglo-Saxon sophistication. Thus, I experienced eye-opening but protected years of *Sturm und Drang* by enjoying an ideal combination of home and freedom.

But my multinational roots and "mixed" sociocultural heritage went deeper than an interest in foreign technology or a few teenage fads. I grew up diglossically in Swiss and Standard German, which are mutually unintelligible, and had many years of formal and intensive instruction in German, English, French, and Latin. I heard all these languages (except the latter) and others spoken at home, as my parents regularly received guests from other parts of Europe, the United States, and elsewhere. My parents also adopted a Tibetan boy, who attracted the family's entire attention and through whom I became acquainted with a sizable Tibetan refugee community in Switzerland. My older sister and her part-Chinese boyfriend introduced me to Chinese food, including the use of chopsticks, and to Asian designs. Moreover, my "foreign" fathers exposed me to liberal political ideas and alternative interpretations of both past and current world events. In fact, dinner-table conversations in my family have often included discussions of politics, religion, and other controversial topics, which, over a glass of wine, could occasionally become rather spirited.

Whereas "the grass across the fence often appeared greener" to me, I also learned early that the big wide world was not always so rosy. A major event in recent history to leave a deep impression on me, as if I had experienced it in person, was World War II, which regularly assumed reality through my family's memories of it: my father's encounters with Nazi terror in his native country, my mother's and my maternal aunts' accounts of the bombing of the lake's German shore by the Allies at night (including their fear of errant shells hitting the Swiss side), and my stepfather's unpretentious, but all the more impressive, descriptions of his experiences as an Allied soldier on duty in Europe. These recollections gained in reality from occasional visits to the neighboring Federal Republic, where the destruction of World War II still was very much evident through the 1960s. War has remained one of the most terrifying events for me until today, which is why I could not develop any enthusiasm for my (involuntary) military service in the Swiss army.

With my multinational roots, I increasingly came to understand myself as a citizen of Europe rather than of Switzerland. The cosmopolitan and liberal perspective that I have enjoyed and have taken for granted at home has always appeared to me the only valid answer to today's many transnational problems such as war, economic exploitation, and environmental destruction. In frequent disagreement with popular opinion, I have argued that Switzerland's international responsibilities could not be limited to membership in a few "nonpolitical" international organizations concerned with emergency aid and relief, economic development, science, or culture (such as the International Red Cross as well as selected European and United Nations organizations). My own international roots have specifically led me to support an active role for Switzerland in Europe's unification and full membership in the United Nations beyond minimalist international agreements. I have even taken the unorthodox position that my native country should take the initiative and leadership in Europe's political unification. This plan has seemed to be the sole feasible long-term solution for a peaceful Europe. The alternatives in which the European Community either dictates the conditions for Switzerland's eventually unavoidable admission to the union or leaves the country isolated like a hole in the center of the continent are realistically unacceptable, as an increasing number of Swiss citizens and government officials have apparently come to recognize in a recent *Euro-Initiative.* The common claim by fellow citizens to Switzerland's political neutrality has long appeared to me a weak argument, questionable by a long history of partiality as evident, for example, in dubious international trades of arms and various unconstitutional approaches to NATO.

I today envision an international confederation of states analogous to the national one of the Swiss cantons as a model for a unified Europe. Such an association of European states would be characterized by a modern liberal constitution, a political system of direct democracy (including the right to referenda and initiatives), an explicitly multilingual and multicultural constituency, and circumscribed federalism. I would also hope for such a unified Europe to assume true armed neutrality, committed to nonoffensive international politics.

My views have corresponded to what Adolf Muschg has perceptively described in *Die Schweiz am Ende—Am Ende die Schweiz* (1990), a collection of essays on Switzerland's recent history and future role in a unified Europe, whose title translates as "Switzerland at the End—In the End Switzerland." Yet, counter to official tenet and public opinion, the author has argued that what makes Switzerland (including its political system of direct democracy) unique is not Tellian in tradition; in fact is not even Swiss in origin. Instead, it is the product of foreign immigrants such as Friedrich Engels, who completed the civil revolution of 1848 in Switzerland. Hence, Muschg has proposed that, to maintain its identity, Switzerland must open its doors to Europe, just as it could serve as a multilingual and multicultural model for a European confederation.

In my search for a more intact world, I had originally had in mind a political system for Europe like that of the United States of America, only to switch to a Muschgian view over the years. But the United States has continued to exert on me a strong fascination in other ways, especially for its size and multiethnic composition. Blues and jazz have mesmerized me not only for their artistic value but also because of their social implications; in a world of so much conflict, this music has offered an alternative art by successfully blending different cultural traditions into a new "international" one.[4] Following a long romantic tradition in Europe, I developed an interest in the native population of the United States. Native Americans had already played an important role in my youth, shaped by juvenile fiction of little literary or ethnographic value, only to grow beyond the interest of boyhood into a serious anthropological concern.

Eventually, I had an opportunity for overseas travel on student exchange programs—first to Great Britain during a summer while still in *Gymnasium* and then to the United States after I had obtained my Swiss university-entrance degree, the *Maturität* (a cognate of English *maturity*). My visits to both countries proved exciting beyond all expectations. While living with local families for several weeks, I could experience and participate in their daily lives and could also undertake some traveling, especially in the United States. On a visit among Caddo in Oklahoma, I also came to meet Native Americans for the first time.

In the fall of the same year, I entered the Universität Basel, which with its international atmosphere seemed a sample international community. For my major, I chose ethnology, which not only provided a better understanding of cultural differences and seemed to hold all the answers to the world's problems but also fed my enduring curiosity about the alien and different, especially Native Americans. There kept lingering in my mind the question of what had really happened to the Native Americans, so often presumed to be absorbed into modern American society or else extinct. My early university studies thus stimulated an interest in acculturation, which I have always understood as a reciprocal (if often uneven) process between members of two or more societies rather than a one-way street. I developed a particular fascination for the creative ways by which communities merged elements of their own traditions with foreign influences into new creations (as in jazz music), and I soon turned to such phenomena as cultural-revitalization movements among Native Americans and native peoples of the Pacific. When I expanded my academic horizon to include linguistics, my interest translated into a fascination for language contact and contact languages including pidgins and creoles.

In considering all these topics, I never forgot my own multicultural background, and I like to think today that it provided me with awareness for cultural differences as well as mutual accommodations in acculturation.

MOVE TO AND RESIDENCE IN THE UNITED STATES

My university studies in Switzerland instilled in me a growing desire to return to the United States for the purpose of gaining special expertise in Native American ethnology and doing an ethnographic field study in a native community.

In the fall of 1972, I transferred to the University of Wisconsin at Madison as a special graduate student in anthropology with generous financial support by a private Basel foundation. Originally, I had no intention to obtain a degree in the United States. But as I met the university's academic qualifications in spite of fundamental differences between the Swiss and American systems of higher education, I took the opportunity to pursue a Ph.D. in this country rather than returning to Switzerland after a year or two of special studies.

While solidifying my interest in cultural anthropology, I expanded my studies to linguistics, especially the topic of language in culture and society. A major concern of mine has since been ethnologically defined models of language change that incorporate a broad range of socio-cultural factors. Much of my research has subsequently focused on the applicability of sociolinguistic models derived from the study of pidgins and creoles to Native American languages. Drawing on both field and archival research, my dissertation project consisted of a sociolinguistic and ethnohistorical study of Mobilian Jargon, a Native American pidgin of the lower Mississippi valley (Drechsel 1979, 1986).

Likewise, far beyond my original plans, I had met during the 1973 Linguistic Institute at the University of Michigan a woman who did not remain just a casual acquaintance but became a close friend and eventually my wife. Rather than returning to Europe after obtaining my Ph.D., I followed an academic career in this country, again by invitation rather than by plan. One position provided the stepping stone for another. Over the years, I lived in Georgia, Louisiana, and Oklahoma aside from Wisconsin and other parts of the upper Midwest. On visits to the Atlantic and West coasts, I have moreover become acquainted with both the city and state of New York, the New England area, Texas, northern California, and Hawai'i. Although my research has focused on Native Americans and I have visited various Great Lakes, Southern, and Plains communities, my field projects have also acquainted me with many of their non-Native American neighbors such as Acadians ("Cajuns") and blacks in southern Louisiana. Over the years, I have encountered people of other ethnic groups and social backgrounds in various circumstances—Americans of diverse European ancestries, African Americans, native Hawaiians, and Japanese, Chinese, and Filipino communities in Hawai'i. Currently, I again reside in Hawai'i, where my wife, a native Hawaiian, and I moved after several years of residence on the mainland.

I have now lived in the United States for some twenty years, during which I have pursued a variety of sociolinguistic and ethnohistorical research topics. At the same time, the larger society has not escaped my attention as I have become familiar with several areas and different communities. These have served as context for my personal experiences in this country and my ethnographic observations. I have also gained many valuable insights about U.S. society from teaching anthropology and linguistics at four state universities for more than ten years. The students' reactions to different and strange peoples as well as to their foreign teacher have revealed much about themselves and their society.

I have now been farther away from my original home than I ever intended or imagined to be. Having lived in the United States since the summer of 1972, I have also spent almost half of my life in this country. Yet I have not taken root beyond the acquisition of permanent residency. Whereas the U.S. Office of Immigration and Naturalization considers me an immigrant, I have not felt like a settler. Obtaining American citizenship has not been on my mind—not for any reason of personal variance or animosity but solely because of my identity. With all my interest in Native Americans and my appreciation for life in this country, I have remained a European at heart throughout these years. In this, my two fathers have probably served as role models, who—although residents in Switzerland—have always maintained their foreign citizenships and identities.

From a sociological perspective, I have remained a visitor, albeit an extended one, as is characteristic of academics and other highly mobile professionals. The purpose of my move to the United States was purely professional. Unlike so many preceding immigrants to this country, I did not have to escape from economic disaster, political persecution, religious oppression, or some other misfortune that would leave me with little or no hope, let alone desire, of ever returning home. I have thus had the luxury of escaping the intrinsic social pressures for settling and starting a new life in the United States that "true" immigrants experience when leaving behind their native countries.

In maintaining my European identity, I have continued looking at modern U.S. society from an outside perspective; hence I do not claim my observations to be emic. I also contend that, as a visitor, I have not necessarily shared the amenable attitudes of true immigrants, eager to start a new life, to settle down, to embrace their new environments without reservations, and perhaps even to forget their original home.

However, I would not make any claim to objectivity if such were possible in the first place; I fully recognize the influence of my own sociocultural environment and personal experiences on my perspective but in different ways. These have indeed affected my interactions with Americans. In all my gratitude for their hospitality, I have maintained differing views; with all due respect for my hosts, I have also taken the liberty to disagree with them. While occasionally critical, my observations are intended in honesty and ultimately remain sympathetic.

RECEPTION IN THE UNITED STATES

It would not have occurred to me to mention my "visitor" status had people in this country not again and again presumed me to be in political or other exile from my native country. Quite unexpectedly, many Americans—usually nonacademics and middle-class people of European ancestry—apparently thought of me as a refugee of some sort when they learned of my foreign origin. They often assumed that I had moved to the United States to escape a repressive society, to enjoy free enterprise, and to pursue "the American Dream." Amusingly, many Americans have also thought—quite erroneously—that, as a foreigner, I did not pay local or federal taxes, even if I drew a regular income from an American employer and a government institution such as a state university. This and other similar privileges again were presumably due to my special status as a refugee.

What has probably made my hosts' attempt at determining my national origin more difficult is my foreign accent, which has occasional British features but is otherwise undefinable to many Americans. Most apparently do not hear a remnant German accent that I notice in linguistic recordings of my own speech, and instead are primarily aware of Briticisms in my English, which still reflects the influence of my Swiss secondary education with BBC English as a model.

Judging by my English speech, many Americans have hence assumed my native country to be either England or—more often—one of its former colonies and new commonwealth associates. Numerous people have regularly guessed my home to be in Australia, which I first assumed they had simply confused with (German-speaking) Austria, but their references to "down under" in further conversation left little doubt about their intentions. Several Americans have also wondered whether I came from India—possibly because they have noticed a greater range in pitch in my English, similar to that of southern Asia when compared to American English, although the intonation patterns of the English spoken by East Indians and Swiss differ substantially from each other. In an extraordinary instance of national misidentification, a foreign-exchange officer at an Oklahoma bank, where I ordered a draft in Swiss francs drawn on a bank in Geneva, thought of me as the son of white settlers in Swaziland. Such preconceptions about my origin perhaps explain why some Americans have thought of me as a refugee.[5]

Americans have revealed other misconceptions about my origins. Many people have again and again confused my native country with Sweden, in which case conversation inevitably turned to free sex, democratic socialism, and cars. Once identified as a citizen of the Alpine republic in central Europe, I have encountered various other stereotypes. Americans have often thought of me as the son of wealthy watchmakers, chocolatiers, or financiers—with a secret bank account at home and on some private business in this country. That neither my parents nor I have been engaged in any of these enterprises or that Switzerland might have more diverse industries (such as precision instruments and machinery including sophisticated weaponry, chemicals and pharmaceuticals, jewelry, textiles, fashion, and foods other than milk products) has apparently crossed the mind of but a few of my hosts. The esoteric study of America's native peoples and their languages has appeared to them as even a stranger reason for leaving Europe.

When the discussion dealt with Europe, Americans have frequently expressed admiration for its "cultural wealth" as evident in fine cuisine, high fashion, time-honored architecture, distinct arts, and a rich history. In recent years, conversations have also dealt with topics of new technology as related to automobiles, trains, and airplanes. Many Americans have even expressed some sort of cultural insecurity or inferiority in relation to Europeans, with which I have taken issue—usually in vain.

I first interpreted such reactions simply as part of initial courtesies and relation building by Americans, especially in conversation with a European such as myself. But I have found the same indications to apply if my conversational partners had no previous knowledge of my European ancestry and in fact assumed my native country to be outside of Europe. Their surprise has usually been all the greater learning my true origin.

While appreciating approval for things of which Europeans and Swiss in particular can justifiably be proud, I have more often felt overwhelmed by Americans' praise to the extent of feeling embarrassed, for my understanding of Europe's modern history ranging from my parents' memories of World War II to my own experience of more recent events could hardly justify so much acclaim. To such expressions of enthusiasm, whether or not genuine, I have struggled to find an appropriate response. Neither full approval nor silence has seemed appropriate, and outright disagreements have appeared outright improper. Polite arguments suggesting that North America's history is equally rich, if only different, and that it in fact reveals greater diversity than Europe's have usually dispersed in the wind. Probably worst among my various reactions have been my tongue-in-cheek agreements. Those Americans not familiar with a kind of devil's advocate teasing, especially nonacademics, have regularly misunderstood such responses. I guess that they also interpreted them as typically arrogant European, and no follow-up explanations could alter their opinion. I have observed similar situations of unease or even miscommunications between Americans and other Europeans, which have in fact served as a telling mirror of my own interactions. Nowadays, I usually respond in a mumbled mixture of approval and disapproval as an unsatisfactory way out.

My experiences with Americans' perception of Europeans and reaction toward them have inadvertently made me wonder how Americans perceive themselves in sociocultural terms. In particular, I began wondering whether Americans socioculturally attempted to be Europeans instead of themselves and whether such behavior revealed an unconscious awareness of cultural differences that they did not recognize otherwise.

"AMERICA" AS A HOME OF TRANSPLANTED EUROPEANS?

From my informal conversations with many Americans of all ethnic and social origins over the years and on various occasions including fieldwork, class, and parties, there has indeed emerged a widely shared picture: a *perception* by Americans of themselves as culturally "Europeans transplanted to the New World," albeit politically independent.

Usually, phenotypically white Americans have cited their European ancestry and have neglected to mention non-European elements in their family history, as if their ancestors had lived in total isolation from their various non-European neighbors. I cannot recall any European American voluntarily sharing information about any of their non-European ancestry. Only on learning about my interest in Native Americans have some people occasionally come forth and made a reference to a Native American predecessor, many by responding that their grandmother had been Cherokee. In most instances, their answer was rather stereotypical, and they could not provide any further details about their Native American background such as their grandmother's name, language, and so on. No white American has ever admitted to any African elements in his or her ancestry although such are evident throughout the South.

On the other hand, if the physical appearance of Americans revealed any obvious non-European ethnicity as in skin color, facial features, or hair, they would usually provide an explanation of considerable detail about their Native American, African, Asian, or other ancestors. Many "non-European" Americans, among them Native Americans and African Americans of Louisiana, have freely shared information about their European descent along with their non-European and have done so without denying their Indian or African identity. Similarly, kin of my wife's mother, most of them phenotypically Hawaiians or Asians, see themselves in part as descendants of a nineteenth-century German or possibly Dutch settler by the name of Elderts, and they even attribute specific family characteristics to his ancestry. Also indicative of U.S. Americans' view of their own society as fundamentally European is the widespread concern about the change in ethnic composition of the United States in favor of a growing nonwhite population, as reflected most eminently in a recent issue of the national news magazine *Time* (9 April 1990).

There are various other indications for Americans' cultural identification with Europe. Historically, the United States would not have shown such an extensive commitment to fighting two world wars in Europe in the first half of the current century had the country not felt some sense of close kinship with it. Likewise, neither the American public nor the government would have paid as much attention to the recent developments in Europe, quite possibly at the expense of the Third World. In terms of their geographical perspective, the urban area on the upper Atlantic Coast area (including Boston, New York, and Washington among others) has remained the economic and political hub of the United States in spite of major economic problems and overall has sustained an Atlantic orientation with a focus on Europe. The federal government, Wall Street, and the United Nations as indications of political and economic power have retained their offices on the East Coast and have no immediate intentions to move to California with a corresponding 180-degree switch in orientation. Cities of the same northeastern area have also provided major resources for this country's education, the arts, and—in many significant ways—industry. By their mere location, other major urban centers east of the Rocky Mountains such as Chicago, Atlanta, and New Orleans have had long-standing ties with the Atlantic and, by extension, Europe. New Orleans' ties to the Caribbean and to Central and South America and its close link to the Pacific via the Panama Canal cannot hide its partiality toward Europe, especially its former colonial master France.

There are obvious exceptions to my generalization about a basic European orientation by much of U.S. society, but they actually strengthen my argument further in the form of negative evidence. Traditional Native Americans, various other minority groups, and recent immigrant communities such as Vietnamese maintain their own distinct identities and are perceived by the larger public as socioculturally marginal. Apparently they do not "count" until they are presumed to be successfully acculturated to the "European" way of life. Then, there are the states west of the Plains, especially the West Coast and even more so Hawai'i, with their orientation toward the Pacific and Asia. But they have not succeeded in fundamentally changing the established perception of the United States as a culturally "European" nation. While competing with the East Coast in terms of education, popular culture (such as film and music), and industry (for example, computers), California has yet to become the nation's hub in international politics and economy. Much of Hawai'i is a prime exception by its mere geography, island ecology, and history, revealing distinct Polynesian traditions and Asian influences, and as such has remained unique among the fifty states. Ultimately, not even the islands have been immune to Europe's lures, as when the state's governor John Waihe'e, the first of part-Hawaiian ancestry, visited various European countries in 1989 for the purpose of expanding and improving business contacts and when state officials make repeated references to the islands' long-standing ties in trade, education, and culture to Europe. A conspicuous sample of such European influence is the Royal Hawaiian Band with its distinct Prussian accessories and a substantial repertoire of German tunes, a carefully maintained institution going back to Hawai'i's imperial era in the nineteenth century. The Pacific Age, until recently predicted to be just around the corner, still seems quite far away.

The widespread, overall cultural identification of U.S. Americans with Europe has obvious roots in this country's history—the European's dominance in the colonization and historical settlements of North America, and the United States in particular, accompanied by the subordination, enslavement, and extermination of non-European peoples (natives, Africans, and Asians). On the other hand, there is a common but vague notion that, after Columbus's "discovery," Europeans came to the Americas, found a mostly empty land, settled, proliferated, established their first democracy, and eventually expanded—all presumably under God's directions. Not even the major events that people recognize in U.S. history, namely the American Revolution and—in the South—the Civil War, have ever put into question the separatists' presumed cultural roots in Europe. The American Revolution merely severed the country's political dependency on England, and the Civil War would at best have led to another independent political entity in North America in people's minds without changing its fundamentally "European" sociocultural orientation. As I have found from conversations with past and present students as well as professionals, orthodox history has continued presenting the United States, one-time colonies of European powers, as a historical extension of Europe. When stripped of names and ethnic identifiers, conventional accounts of American history read just like historical tales of European history such as my Appenzeller ancestral tales or the Swiss' very own Wilhelm Tell legend. Yet, just as I along with other Swiss cannot claim a single line of ancestry, U.S. Americans are not simply transplanted Europeans but share a history of multiple cultural traditions.

A EUROPEAN'S PERCEPTION OF U.S. SOCIETY

Myths of origin as gathered by anthropologists among peoples around the globe have raised questions about the ethnographic and historical validity of such accounts. Thinking about how U.S. Americans perceive themselves has stimulated reflections of my own about this country, in which I have examined my experiences and my observations from an anthropological perspective.

In contrast to their own perception, Americans have in fact appeared to me as socioculturally different from Europeans since my early youth and have been distinct from the British as well, although for all practical purposes they speak the same language. My first impressions were based largely on juvenile stereotypes. Yet as I came to rely on my own observations and experiences while living in the United States, my view changed to one of this country as socioculturally even more unique, that is, distinctly American and correspondingly less European.

After the initial excitement about the United States' width, diversity, and novelty had worn down, I also experienced moments of boredom, frustration, and even homesickness in this country. In spite of exciting new American dishes such as bigger and juicier cheeseburgers, many delicious pies, spicy Blackened Redfish, and fine Mexican cuisine, I have regularly longed for a "hearty" *Röschti* instead of its American counterpart of onionless and half-fried hashbrowns, various Swiss cheeses (of which there is not just what Europeans identify as Emmentaler but a great diversity of others), a glass of Fendant (a dry Swiss white wine, rarely exported to the United States because of its limited production), or simply a "warm" beer with a "spicy" flavor. On the other hand, I have missed a regular spirited discussion of topics close to my heart (like philosophy, politics, or history) in place of gracious dinner-table conversations on the weather, the job, or sports, the latter for which I have not developed any more enthusiasm since my youth. Americans', and especially American men's, preoccupation with sports, as evident from their pervasive presence in high schools and colleges and from all their attention in the media, seems distinctly American. In contrast, a German newsweekly that I regularly consult, *Die Zeit,* and other European newspapers carry no section on sports or discuss them solely as sociohistorical phenomena on rare occasions. The continued avoidance of the metric system as official measurement in this country renders it likewise unique. But most significant, there is something of a surviving

Wild West mentality as demonstrated by Americans' rejection of a national gun law and support for the death penalty.

Such experiences of American sociocultural distinctness have not been uniquely my own but are shared by other Europeans and foreigners because of their different sociocultural backgrounds. In all these instances, it has helped little that I had been exposed to U.S. American culture in childhood and while still in Europe. Also, I could hardly deny my emotions, positive or negative, about my new surroundings, although as an anthropologist I can rationalize about such differences and my reactions toward them. Drawing on my own cross-cultural experiences, I would actually doubt any anthropologist or other social scientist who—however marginal to his or her own original home—claimed immunity from any similar reactions about a new social environment. I would suspect that he or she was either dishonest or mentally ill.

Yet to some social scientists, my experiences may reflect minimal or superficial sociocultural differences between the United States and Europe and would not justify an ethnological interpretation of American society as anything other than fundamentally European. After all, so might go the argument, I could experience differences of a similar kind in another part of Europe or possibly even within Switzerland in another language area. In actuality, there are more substantial sociocultural differences between the United States and Europe, albeit underlying and less obvious.

A good but rarely cited example is humor. After twenty some years, I still wonder about much American humor as presented in comic strips, on television, and in films. There are some aspects of "Doonesbury," "M*A*S*H," Bill Cosby (but not his co-actors) in "The Cosby Show," and Cookie Monster of the Muppets that make me laugh. But I experience little or no amusement in most American comedies, especially slapstick humor, that an entire audience in a movie theater may find hilarious. Instead, and to the embarrassment of my wife or other American company, I am often entertained by scenes that, as judged by the audience's reaction, apparently were not intended to be absurd. A drastic example of such comedy might even be sermons by fundamentalist television preachers, were I not fully aware of their questionable motivation and practices. Conversely, my and other Europeans' sense of humor has usually resulted in bewilderment among my wife and most of my American friends. For this reason, I have consciously avoided making jokes, especially in the classroom, for fear of simply not being understood or inadvertently offending my audience. Quite unexpectedly and to my pleasant surprise, I have occasionally made my classes laugh when I had absolutely no intention of making a joke.

American humor need not escape me for linguistic reasons, for I have had considerably less difficulty in following British humor as available in magazines like *Punch* or on television broadcasts such as "Monty Python's Flying Circus" and "Spitting Image." If the linguistic argument applied, the reverse would in fact hold true because I have now had considerably less exposure to British than American English. Instead, I believe there is a nonlinguistic difference in the form of a much stronger political dimension in my and many other Europeans' understanding of humor as compared to that of Americans, who regularly shun such in accord with their avoidance of politics and religion as suitable topics of dinner-table conversations. There may yet be another, more substantial difference between their definition of the absurd, which I am not prepared to pinpoint here. However, our mutual reactions have reminded me time and again that these sociocultural differences are real even if they escape full description.

An even more significant example of characteristic American culture in my own experience has been blues and jazz music. Besides giving me a great deal of personal pleasure and excitement, this art form has pointed the way to my perspective of the United States as socioculturally American rather than European. Often misrepresented as uniquely black American, blues and jazz music has obvious African and European roots and is an exemplary representation of what in my mind has been distinctly U.S. American—a creative integration of diverse cultural traditions into a new form of art. If seen in their larger sociohistorical context, including their impact on modern "classical" as well as popular music, blues and jazz music no longer remains that apparently marginal tradition surviving in more or less stereotypical presentations of Dixieland music in New Orleans' French Quarter, in sterilized dance music presented as swing, in a few select and smoky clubs of New York City or San Francisco, or on "elitist" public radio stations.[6] That blues and jazz music has long had a worldwide impact and that there may now exist a more lively scene of jazz music outside the United States alters little in my argument and only demonstrates its attraction as a result of its creative power. It has proved to be a great disappointment not to hear as much jazz in concerts and the media as I had expected. I also remain astonished about how little public recognition modern jazz musicians such as the late John Coltrane have enjoyed, although his characteristic phrasing in tenor and soprano saxophone playing reappears in imitations throughout today's popular music.

Rather than dismissing blues and jazz music as a sociocultural epiphenomenon, I hold it as a key to our understanding of U.S. American culture, representative of the neglect, if not disregard, of non-European traditions or a reinterpretation of these, if recognized, in terms of some vague European history. This typical American art form has in fact inspired my interest in acculturation in general, which has extended all the way into the ethnology of Native Americans and into anthropological linguistics, as evident in my research on pidgins and creoles. The example of blues and jazz is only one among many that make me think of the United States as a society fundamentally different from Europe in spite of obvious and many significant historical interconnections.

Just as Dixieland is not simply brass music performed by a European military marching band, American society is not Europe transplanted to North America; rather, it is a historical almagam of diverse cultural influences including Native American, European, African, Asian, and others.

Among various instances, there are some that reflect distinct Native American flavors. Usually interpreted as a Pilgrim or even Judeo-Christian holiday and celebrated with full fervor, the prime American holiday of Thanksgiving is by all indications Native American in its roots—in terms not only of a typical menu consisting of corn, sweet potato, turkey, cranberry sauce, and pumpkin pie but also of the overall idea of expressing gratitude around fall. Thanksgiving probably was a European immigrants' partial adaptation of the Green Corn Ceremony once widespread among the native peoples of eastern North America, who gave thanks for successful crops of corn in either summer or fall in a kind of new-year celebration (see Witthoft 1949). That most Americans hereby happen to express their gratitude to a Judeo-Christian god today is incidental.

It is tragic that Thanksgiving, whether or not recognized as a Judeo-Christian tradition, has not become an occasion for acknowledgment of the native peoples, to whom this country and the world at large owes so much. When Europeans first set foot onto the North American continent, it was not that vast area of wilderness inhabited by a few "savages" as still imagined in the minds of many history teachers. As archaeologists have demonstrated repeatedly, American history has built on a long and solid prehistory, to which there appear more connections than disruptions in spite of the Europeans' enslavement and systematic genocide of native peoples. In addition to the stereotypical Thanksgiving produce, Native Americans have contributed many other items of food. What would gumbo and many other local dishes of Louisiana be without *filé,* an indigenous spice consisting of pounded sassafras? The indigenous peoples of North America have also made significant contributions to technology, such as the canoe and toboggan as means of transportation, the adobe as insulator, and the pueblo as architectural design. Moreover, the horticultural and agricultural traditions of Native Americans have been the basis for numerous pharmaceutical and chemical products of today, just as much of the modern cultural geography of the United States, including the infrastructure, has built on traditional indigenous settlements, trails, and waterways. Many place names with unconventional spellings, including Mississippi, Wisconsin, Chicago, and numerous others, reflect Native American linguistic influences. *Bayou,* a term that refers to a marshy and sluggish tributary to a river or lake in Louisiana and adjacent states, is not French in origin as we might surmise from its spelling or pronunciation; instead, it derives from Mobilian Jargon or the Chickasaw-Choctaw trade language and ultimately from Choctaw proper, that is, *bayuk* (river, creek). Native

Americans on the Atlantic Coast may even have invested early European settlers with egalitarian, revolutionary ideas of liberty and democracy that their descendants now claim as their own. Acadian ("Cajun") music with its obvious elements of European folk music and blues reveals some characteristic native scales as well. I often wonder whether typical American ball games such as football and baseball do not likewise draw on Indian influences. It has even occurred to me at the risk of unduly stretching my argument that the long American tradition of warm hospitality and generosity may reflect a native heritage. From my ethnohistorical research on Indians of eastern North America, I inadvertently recall the many early accounts of their magnanimity toward Europeans and other immigrants, their open-arms reception and even full adoption of the newcomers into native societies, often culminating in the latter's transculturalization (see Hallowell 1963).

Reflecting my special areas of interest, these examples are but a select and isolated few among many other native influences on American culture that anthropologists and ethnohistorians have recognized for some time (for a recent survey, see Axtell 1981, especially Chapter 10). Yet, whereas the European impact is widely recognized in Native American societies, U.S. Americans—including social scientists and historians—usually neglect or fail to recognize reverse influences in their own society or history except perhaps in negative terms. For this one-sided picture of the United States, Americanist anthropologists and historians bear some responsibility because, in our studies of acculturation and culture change in general, we have yet to give equal and methodical consideration to the question of the indigenous impact on the U.S. American society. Unfortunately, much Americanist ethnological and ethnohistorical discussion has remained superficial in this respect by listing single examples of influences, as I have done above, or by focusing on selective borrowings rather than taking into account the overall process. It is sad but indicative that, for instance, Volume 4 of the *Handbook of North American Indians,* entitled *History of Indian-White Relations* (Washburn 1988), does not offer a separate, systematic discussion of this question. On the other hand, long-needed popular publications such as Jack Weatherford's *Indian Givers* (1988) often present oversimplified and tenuous reasoning. Unfortunately, such studies, although commendable in intention, may only reinforce long-held stereotypes of Native Americans as "the noble savage."

Similar arguments of substantive non-European cultural influences in American society extend to Africans, Hawaiians, and Asians among others, as is evident in food, speech, folklore, music, and so on. From a historical perspective with a time-depth extending back into "prehistory" and with greater attention to ethnic diversity, it becomes increasingly difficult to imagine how the United States could *not* have drawn on or incorporated other, non-European traditions. Orthodox Americanist social science actually owes an explanation of how this country could have remained as European as it is usually presumed. In dealing with this issue, we might open our eyes toward non-European elements in U.S. American history and society.

With proper attention to prehistory, the historic role of non-European peoples, and mutual interethnic acculturation, the United States no longer appears socioculturally as European as commonly assumed. Yet U.S. society is not simply a loose and disorganized mixture of European and non-European cultural elements but a different sociohistorical entity that forms an integrated whole in spite of numerous internal discrepancies, conflicts, and external influences. In other words, U.S. American culture is a *creole,* interpretable in either traditional terms or as a metaphor borrowed from linguistics. In the first instance, a creole can be a person of partial or even predominant European descent, born and raised in America with a tradition of his or her own including distinct non-European influences. *Creole* also refers to the first language of a multilingual community that derives from an interlingual medium technically known as pidgin with characteristically diverse influences from many languages including non-European ones (see, for example, Romaine 1988).

In analogy to the linguistic analysis of creole language and in contrast to related European languages, the sociocultural as well as linguistic similarities between the United States and Europe appear more superficial and their differences correspondingly deeper and more substantial than commonly suggested. The differences refer not only to sociocultural traditions passed on by Native Americans or introduced by immigrants from outside the Americas and Europe but also to newly created, modern American traditions such as blues and jazz music. As in creole languages, such non-European elements are not always obvious or distinct; nevertheless they are not any less real than the widely acknowledged European influences. One reason why they are more difficult to recognize is that they have been submerged in what may superficially appear as a European heritage—in analogy to non-European features in creole languages such as African elements in Caribbean creoles and even in black English or Hawaiian features in Hawaiian creole ("pidgin"). In the latter case, note for instance the characteristic Hawaiian syntactic pattern of predicate and subject in a conventional phrase like "Good da food," not to mention other Hawaiian influences evident, for example, in the vocabulary. A recognition of such underlying differences adds a complementary dimension to our understanding of American history and culture that will make it considerably more diversified and richer.

In short, European traditions have blended with non-European ones into a sociocultural almagam with characteristics and a history unique to U.S. American society. Like America's other historical societies, this country has been substantially different in its culture from Europe even though the latter has selectively adopted various old and new American inventions since its "discovery" of the Western Hemisphere.

THE ETHNOGRAPHIC METAPHOR OF "CIRCUS"

Whereas this can hardly be the place for an ethnography or ethnohistory of the United States, a metaphor—that of "circus"—offers an interpretation of U.S. society in terms of a separate sociocultural entity, as it may *appear* to outsiders. This metaphor solely is a figure of speech or a summary of ethnographic impressions and does not provide an explanation of historical development for any U.S. sociocultural characteristics. This analogy not only draws on experiences and observations of my own but also relies on impressions by fellow foreigners in this country, conservative Native Americans, and other "marginal" Americans, who in spite of substantial sociocultural differences among themselves have shared similar reactions to their larger sociocultural surroundings.

The circus metaphor proposes an intentional association of U.S. society with a typical traveling show including various actors such as clowns and exotic animals performing special acts in a large tent. Further, it is intended to draw on fond childhood memories, which I assume the reader holds. The circus metaphor has no negative, secondary implications in terms of "disorder" or "confusion," nor does it necessarily suggest exclusive applicability to the United States. In reverse, Americans may experience any modern foreign society, including my very own native country, in similar terms.

Principally, the circus metaphor suggests that to outsiders Americans are more "theatrical" in appearance than their common self-image of rationality, business, and science makes them believe. At the same time, U.S. American culture, while remaining strange, is alluring, perhaps even fantastic (in the literal sense) to outsiders, just as the circus world exerts fascination on its audience. Yet aside from this general allegory, U.S. society exhibits numerous specific circuslike traits and includes among them some exotic and esoteric elements.

First, U.S. American culture is youth-focused, as evident in advertising, fashion, and the consumer market at large. Like a circus, Americans constantly appear to be "on tour," as reflected in the rapid changes in fashion, fads, and moods among their younger generations. These changes reveal uncertainty about Americans' sociocultural identity and little of any deeply rooted sense of history, but they also reveal a willingness for social experimentation, comparable to new acts in the ring.

At times, the United States even comes across as a huge Disneyland, which lives in a circus dream world with its newspaper comic strips, television cartoons, the unrealistic world of Hollywood, fantastic toys, and entertainment and theme parks. A distance to reality comes through in the dominant emphasis on "fun" in primary and secondary education with all its attention to sports and nonessential areas such as military-preparation programs, usually at the expense of basic academics. There are still other aspects that reflect a dream world: school and military parades; elaborate graduation ceremonies and parties, including such extravagant features as the students' rental of fancy limousines;[7] much clamor and hoopla accompanying sports events with the raising of flags, the singing of anthems, public invocations, and performances by mascots and cheerleading troupes; and political gatherings with all their show and pomp.

Like the circus as a small world in itself, U.S. American society has exhibited a kind of island mentality, as reflected in its isolation from the larger natural and social environment. There is the continuing reliance on natural resources as if they were limitless. The country's weak or absent commitment to dealing with other major issues, ranging from a national health policy and public education to public transportation and the balancing of the national budget, serves as an example of withdrawal. An island mentality further comes forth in the nation's failed adoption of international standards or its refusal to recognize any international authority (such as the International Court in Den Haag) unless convenient. Even the widespread use of the term *America* in media, education, and the public to refer specifically to the United States rather than the entire hemisphere is a linguistic reflection of unfortunate insensitivity to the country's neighbors, close and distant. From this perspective, the so-called "open" society paradoxically appears quite closed.

Corresponding to magic and other "unreal" acts in a circus, U.S. society exhibits much behavior related to the make-believe or supernatural domain. In light of the constitutionally granted separation of church and state in this country, I have always been surprised about the great permeation of religion in modern U.S. society as evident in prayers or invocations at many government and public-school events, whose appropriateness has usually remained unchallenged without any action by the American Civil Liberties Union. The contrast to my own social background is all the more striking in light of the fact that Switzerland and other countries that do not recognize a strict separation of church and state make far less reference to the supernatural on public occasions.

Yet the wonderworld of the United States with its "circus" orientation has also been the source of much creativity. Americans have obviously demonstrated true imagination and pioneer spirit in the arts and sciences, technology and industry, and other forms of human expression. Examples are so numerous as to make a selection difficult. Yet in a random choice of just a few, there come to mind not only music as in blues and jazz but also national parks, architecture, suspension bridges, J-boats, computers, and space exploration. In their youthful spirit, Americans have moreover surprised me again and again with their seemingly unlimited generosity, ingenuity, and optimism.

Hence, there remains fascination for this country comparable to that of children for the circus. Just as American youngsters abroad feel deprived of the many "fun" things that they had available at home, children of foreigners in this country often have a difficult time returning to their native country and adjusting to what they consider a meager and boring life once they have tasted the "forbidden fruit" and "the greener grass across the fence." This observation by no means applies just to societies with restrictive political or religious ideologies, but to liberal ones of Europe as well. This "dream-world" orientation also exerts an extraordinary fascination on grown-ups from far and wide. I suspect that, on a long-term visit to Europe, I would similarly miss many of the amenities that I have come to enjoy in this country.

CONCLUSION

Rather than leading me astray and into an academic dead end, my interest in Native Americans, their languages, and their societies has led me to a different understanding of the United States, if perhaps via a detour. On the basis of my own multicultural background and through my studies, I have gained a broader perspective of U.S. society and a valuable dimension that might otherwise have escaped me—the country's creole history, including a substantial non-European heritage as exemplified here primarily by its Native American traditions but evident in others such as blues and jazz. Their study inadvertently offers a more comprehensive understanding of American society and history in anthropological terms, which I have interpreted in terms of the metaphor of "circus," an ethnographic profile of U.S. American society from an outsider's perspective.

There even is a moral, although hardly a new one, in this story: Americans may and should be proud of their almagam heritage and their creole history and need not pretend or attempt to be Europeans. On the other hand, non-Americans, including Europeans, must recognize Americans on their own sociocultural terms. A better mutual understanding of cultural differences between Americans and Europeans obviously is a necessity in our rapidly changing relationship and desire for true peace.

Notwithstanding substantial cultural differences from Europe, the United States also remains of interest for comparison as the functional model of a modern multiethnic, multistate society to an emerging unified Europe because of their sociopolitical and economic similarities— better than any other modern, multistate and multiethnic society such as the Union of Soviet Socialist Republics, the People's Republic of China, India, or Brazil. With the United States' previous experiences as a modern multiethnic, multistate society to guide Europe, a unified Europe has the benefit of avoiding major errors in national policies on health, environment, public education, infrastructure including public transportation, and languages, for which Europe ought to be grateful. Commission of similar errors by European nations thus has become much less excusable.

Yet the United States need not serve solely as a negative sample but can still stand as a model with its constitution, many environmental policies, higher education, ingenuity in computer and aerospace technology, and artistic creativity. Certain areas of this country, such as Hawai'i, may also illustrate ethnically diverse communities with substantial social balance and comparatively little discrimination or interethnic strife, which must become a major concern to Europe with its increasing ethnic diversity resulting from a growing immigrant population. Like Americans, Europeans must learn to accept and recognize the increasing creolization of their society with multiple, diverse traditions as a creative development in their future. *E pluribus unum—et plures in uno!*

NOTES

1. I dedicate this essay to my parents—my mother, Rita Hubbard-Bänziger (Swiss), my late father, Armin Drechsel (German), and my stepfather, Stanley L. Hubbard (American), all of whom have significantly shaped my life. I also wish to recognize three major teachers of mine, who happen to represent the same cultural traditions as my parents: the late Hans Ehrenzeller, Meinhard Schuster, and William W. Elmendorf. Furthermore, I must acknowledge the *Werenfels-Fonds der Freiwilligen Akademischen Gesellschaft der Stadt Basel,* whose generous support made possible my dream to study in the United States and built the foundation for much of what was to follow. I also thank my wife, Teresa Haunani Makuakāne-Drechsel, and my Indian colleague, Jaishree Odin, for many helpful suggestions.

2. I recognize that, in presenting autobiographical information, I run the danger of adding a metatwist that ideally requires closer examination as well. But this issue will not receive any further consideration here.

3. Tell is a mythical and literary figure who according to legend shot an apple from his son's head in challenging Austrian usurpers in the thirteenth century and who has served as a patriotic symbol of independence for Switzerland until today.

4. From this perspective, the popular cousins of blues and jazz, namely rock and roll, beat music, and their modern descendants, have mostly appeared melodically pale and rhythmically sterile to me.

5. If in short encounters I did not wish to present a long and complicated explanation about my origins or the reasons for my coming to this country and if I made a conscious attempt at avoiding Briticisms in my speech, I could identify myself with Wisconsin or the upper Great Lakes area, at least in the South, without anybody taking exception or challenging me. Actually, there are formerly German-speaking communities in the upper Midwest (including Swiss-American ones such as

New Glarus in Wisconsin) that have maintained more or less of a distinct German or Swiss accent in their English. Similarly, there are communities of Scandinavian ancestry that exhibit the distinct intonation patterns of their first languages with a greater range in pitch that is similar to mine in some ways.

6. In analogy, we can extend the same reasoning to corresponding musical traditions in other parts of American such as reggae in Jamaica and samba and bossa nova in Brazil.

7. Graduation ceremonies obviously are a form of initiation rites, which seem to reach a peak with high school students. Afterward, the nature and extent of graduation festivities seem to be inversely related to the value of the student's degree.

REFERENCES

AXTELL, JAMES
1981   The European and the Indian. Essays in the Ethnohistory of Colonial North America. Oxford: Oxford University Press.

DARNELL, REGNA
1990   Edward Sapir: Linguist, Anthropologist, Humanist. Berkeley: University of California Press.

DRECHSEL, EMANUEL J.
1979   Mobilian Jargon: Linguistic, Sociocultural, and Historical Aspects of an American Indian *lingua franca*. Doctoral dissertation, Department of Anthropology, University of Wisconsin-Madison. Ann Arbor: University Microfilms International.
1986   Speaking "Indian" in Louisiana. Linguists Trace the Remnants of a Native American Pidgin. Natural History 95 (9): 4–13.

GONSETH, MARC-OLIVIER, ED.
1989–   Images de la Suisse/Schauplatz Schweiz. Ethnologica Helvetica 13/14.
1990   Berne: Schweizerische Ethnologische Gesellschaft.

HALLOWELL, A. IRVING
1963   American Indians, White and Black: The Phenomenon of Transculturalization. Current Anthropology 4 (5): 519–31.

MUSCHG, ADOLF
1990   Die Schweiz am Ende—Am Ende die Schweiz. Erinnerungen an mein Land vor 1991. Frankfurt am Main: Suhrkamp Verlag.

ROMAINE, SUZANNE
1988   Pidgin and Creole Languages. London: Longman.

SWEET, PAUL. R.
1978/   Wilhelm von Humboldt. A Biography. Volume 1: 1767–1808, Volume 2:
1980   1808–1835. Columbus: Ohio State University Press.

WASHBURN, WILCOMB E., ED.
1988   Handbook of North American Indians. Volume 4: History of Indian-White
        Relations. Washington: Smithsonian Institution.

WEATHERFORD, JACK McIVER
1988   Indian Givers. How the Indians of the Americas Transformed the World.
        New York: Crown Publishers.

WITTHOFT, RACHEL
1949   Green Corn Ceremonialism in the Eastern Woodlands. Occasional Con-
        tributions from the Museum of Anthropology at the University of
        Michigan, No. 13. Ann Arbor: University of Michigan Press.